Women with ADHD 5-in-1

The Evidence-Based Guide to Organize Your Life, Sharpen Focus, Balance Hormones, and Master Emotions, Money and Relationships

Vivian Whitmore

Claim Your Free Bonus

As a thank you for reading, I've put together a powerful digital bonus pack to help you apply what you've learned — even if you only have a few minutes a day.

 Inside you'll find:

✔ Quick-access emotional reset tools
✔ A printable clarity map for focus and purpose
✔ 30 powerful journaling prompts
✔ Daily progress & reflection trackers
✔ A mini affirmation deck for calm and confidence

Access below to download your full bonus pack:

https://livetolearn.lpages.co/vivian-withmore-women-with-adhd-5-in-1-paperback/

Or, scan the QR code

Women with ADHD 5-in-1: The Evidence-Based Guide to Organize Your Life, Sharpen Focus, Balance Hormones, and Master Emotions, Money and Relationships

As a psychologist, I have worked with many women with ADHD, and I am familiar with the many challenges they face in daily life. I found this book to be a comprehensive and empowering resource for women navigating the unique challenges of a disorder that is often underdiagnosed or endured in silence among many women. The author integrates current research with practical strategies, offering readers an evidence-based roadmap to better understand themselves and develop skills that enhance daily functioning.

What distinguishes this work is its holistic perspective. Many ADHD guides focus narrowly on time management or productivity, but this book expands the lens to include hormones, emotional regulation, finances, and relationships—domains that are particularly relevant to women. The author underscores the interplay between fluctuating hormone levels and ADHD symptoms, an area often overlooked in traditional texts, and provides realistic coping tools for these cyclical changes.

The sections on organization and focus are pragmatic, with step-by-step approaches for managing clutter, prioritizing tasks, and creating sustainable systems that align with an individual's strengths rather than forcing rigid external models. Equally valuable are the chapters on mastering emotions and communication, which normalize the struggles women often experience in regulating affect and maintaining interpersonal balance. The financial guidance is another strength, addressing impulsive spending and decision fatigue with concrete, research-informed interventions.

Clinically, I appreciate the balance between validation and empowerment. The author avoids pathologizing, instead framing ADHD as a neurological difference that requires intentional management strategies. The content is relatable, and the evidence cited reassures both clinicians and readers that the recommendations are grounded in science.

Overall, this book is a valuable addition to the ADHD literature. It provides women with practical tools while acknowledging the layered experiences of gender, biology, and environment. I would confidently recommend it to clients and colleagues alike as both a guide on managing ADHD and a source of encouragement.

Carolina Estevez, Psy.D.

Licensed Psychologist

TABLE OF CONTENTS

INTRODUCTION

Attention-Deficit/Hyperactivity Disorder (ADHD) has long been misunderstood, predominantly viewed through a lens shaped by the stereotypical image of a hyperactive young boy. This outdated narrative has created a significant and often devastating gap in understanding, leading to a profound, lifelong struggle for countless women.

For many, ADHD is an unseen battle, a condition that frequently goes under-diagnosed or is misdiagnosed entirely. This diagnostic disparity is largely due to the differences in how ADHD manifests between genders. While men are more likely to exhibit externalized, hyperactive symptoms, such as physical restlessness, excessive talking, and impulsive behaviors, that are easier to notice and lead to an earlier diagnosis, women and girls are more prone to the predominantly inattentive presentation of the disorder.

This inattentive subtype is characterized by internalized struggles, including disorganization, poor time management, forgetfulness, and a pervasive sense of internal restlessness.

The conventional diagnostic criteria, which were largely developed from studies on boys, often fail to capture the nuances of female symptom presentation. Early ADHD research predominantly focused on males, with one study noting that only 21% of participants in the field trials for the DSM-5 diagnostic criteria were girls.

As a result, many diagnostic tools were not designed with women and girls in mind, leading to a limited understanding of female ADHD. Women tend to be diagnosed much later than men, with some studies finding the mean age of diagnosis for females to be up to 28.6 years, compared to 22.7 years for males.

This delayed diagnosis means women often spend years, or even decades, struggling in secret before they receive the proper support. The lack of a diagnosis leaves them without a framework to understand their challenges, leading them to internalize their struggles and blame themselves for their difficulties, a pattern that fuels anxiety, depression, and low self-esteem.

This difference in symptom manifestation, combined with powerful societal expectations for women to be organized, emotionally mature, and calm, creates a pressure to conform that directly conflicts with the core symptoms of ADHD.

This conflict forces many women to engage in a practice known as "masking," where they develop sophisticated compensatory behaviors to hide their struggles and appear "neurotypical" to the outside world.

For instance, a woman might meticulously maintain a façade of punctuality by building in extra time for everything, a strategy she developed to combat her innate time blindness and avoid the social consequences of being late. Another might learn to pretend to take notes in a meeting to hide the fact that she is "zoning out" or has a "thousand-yard stare".

This constant, exhausting effort to appear "non-ADHD" is an invisible burden that leads to a lifetime of internalized shame, anxiety, depression, and a shattered sense of self-worth. This ongoing struggle often means that women are only diagnosed in adulthood, after years of self-blame and the accumulation of co-occurring mental health conditions that were fueled by their untreated and hidden ADHD.

Studies confirm that girls are more likely to mask their symptoms than boys , and this can lead to significant negative consequences on their mental health, social functioning, and academic achievement.

The challenges of living with ADHD for women are not a series of isolated issues; rather, they form a complex, interconnected web. The struggle to maintain organization in Book 1, for example, is not merely about a messy living space, but about the profound mental and emotional toll that mess takes, leading a woman to feel such shame that she may avoid having people over.

Similarly, the difficulties with focus and productivity discussed in Book 2 are not just about getting things done, but about the overwhelming mental fatigue they create and the pervasive sense of being "frenzied" and "frazzled" that so many women with ADHD report.

This emotional and mental exhaustion then directly impacts a woman's ability to manage her hormones in Book 3, which in turn can exacerbate all of her other symptoms. The emotional dysregulation explored in Book 4 and the financial and relational challenges in Book 5 also feed into this cycle.

This guide will provide a comprehensive roadmap to navigate this complex landscape, offering evidence-based strategies to address the five core pillars of living a balanced and fulfilling life with ADHD. By providing a holistic approach, it aims to empower women to not just manage their symptoms but to truly thrive, transforming their unique neurobiology into a source of strength.

The Unique Neurobiology of ADHD in Women

The narrative that ADHD is a less problematic condition in women is outdated and inaccurate. While the core symptoms are similar in both genders, the way they manifest and the long-term impact on women's lives are dramatically different due to a "perfect storm" of internalized symptoms, hormonal fluctuations, and societal pressure. Research is only now beginning to fully explore why ADHD exacts a far greater toll on women.

A key difference is that hyperactivity in women often presents as an internal, rather than external, experience. Instead of fidgeting or running in circles, a woman's mind may be a "L.A. highway with high-speed cars zooming here, there, and everywhere". This internal restlessness and "flight of thoughts" can be just as disruptive as physical hyperactivity, but it is invisible to others and therefore less likely to be noticed or lead to a diagnosis. This can lead to a constant sense of being "frenzied, frazzled, and overwhelmed".

The ADHD brain is also wired differently due to variations in brain structure and neurotransmitter activity, particularly concerning dopamine and norepinephrine. Dopamine is a key neurotransmitter involved in motivation, reward, and executive functions like attention. For individuals with ADHD, the regulation of dopamine is thought to differ, leading to lower levels in the brain's synapses. This can make tasks that are not inherently stimulating or rewarding feel incredibly difficult to initiate and sustain.

The Emotional and Social Toll

For many women, the most debilitating aspect of their ADHD is not inattention, but emotional dysregulation. Research consistently shows that a significant percentage of adults with ADHD struggle to regulate their emotions, and women with the disorder are more likely than men to internalize these struggles, leading to self-blame.

This heightened emotional intensity is a hallmark of the female ADHD experience. A woman may experience emotions that feel "all or nothing" , with a rapid-fire succession of intense emotional states that can lead to being "overwhelmed by even minor hiccups and inconveniences".

This is because the frontal cortex of the ADHD brain, which is responsible for inhibiting big reactions, is often less activated. This can cause a woman to lash out, cry, or spiral into sadness with little warning, a pattern that is often misdiagnosed as a mood disorder.

A particularly painful and pervasive manifestation of this emotional dysregulation is Rejection Sensitive Dysphoria (RSD). While not a formal diagnosis, RSD is a descriptive term for an "extreme emotional responsiveness and anxiety in anticipation of, or in response to, perceived rejection or criticism from others".

For women with ADHD, who have often endured a lifetime of "chronic negative feedback" and a fear of their "perceived failures" being discovered , this can be an immediate, overwhelming emotional pain that feels physically agonizing. This hypersensitivity can make them people-pleasers or perfectionists, but it also makes them more susceptible to suicidal thoughts and self-harm than their male counterparts.

The combination of inattention and emotional dysregulation also takes a significant toll on relationships and friendships. Women with ADHD may struggle to form and maintain friendships, feeling a painful sense of "never fitting in". They may find it difficult to show up on time for social commitments, or to suppress the urge to interrupt in conversation because they fear they will forget what they wanted to say. This can lead to social rejection , and for women who have a greater need for social acceptance and connection than men, this can be particularly devastating.

The Interplay of Hormones and ADHD

A critical and often under-researched factor in the female ADHD experience is the profound impact of hormonal fluctuations throughout a woman's life. While this link has been an anecdotal reality for decades, many women feel their experiences are not "believed" by healthcare professionals.

Research confirms that sex hormones, like estrogen and progesterone, directly influence neurotransmitters like dopamine. Estrogen, in particular, is linked to an increase in dopamine levels. This connection explains why a woman's ADHD symptoms can feel different at various life stages, such as during puberty, the menstrual cycle, perimenopause, and menopause.

For women who menstruate, for example, studies suggest that attention and executive function can worsen in the low-estrogen luteal phase, which is the period leading up to menstruation. This hormonal environment can lead to more pronounced inattention, anxiety, and stress, and can even make a woman's ADHD medication feel less effective.

The intersection of ADHD and Premenstrual Dysphoric Disorder (PMDD), a more severe form of PMS, is also significant, with a high percentage of women with ADHD also experiencing PMDD. The combination of these two conditions can make emotional regulation even more challenging, leading to more pronounced mood swings, irritability, and anger. This understanding of the hormonal link is crucial for developing personalized and effective treatment plans.

For women in midlife, the hormonal shifts of perimenopause and menopause can present a major and often unexpected challenge. As estrogen and progesterone levels decline, underlying ADHD symptoms that a woman has compensated for throughout her life can become unmanageable. Some experts refer to this as an "ADHD squared" effect: the compounding of low estrogen and low dopamine.

The symptoms of menopause, such as "brain fog," memory lapses, and difficulty with concentration, often mirror the symptoms of ADHD, making it difficult to differentiate between the two conditions and leading to a confusing and frustrating experience.

The Daily Cost of Unmanaged ADHD

The collective toll of these unmanaged symptoms can feel like a daily race to avoid disaster. This is often referred to as the "ADHD tax," a measurable cost that living with the condition can impose over a lifetime.

In the realm of personal finances, ADHD symptoms directly contribute to challenges. Studies show that people with ADHD have lower savings and higher debt, often remaining financially dependent on their families well into adulthood. The impulsivity that can drive spontaneous purchases and the time blindness that leads to late payments are direct consequences of ADHD-related executive function challenges. A woman with ADHD may also struggle to set and stick to a budget or to consistently organize bills and other financial paperwork.

Daily life can feel overwhelming, with even simple chores becoming a source of stress. A woman may find that unwashed dishes and laundry pile up, and she may dislike having people over due to the mess. The pervasive sense of disorganization can lead her to waste time looking for everyday items or to feel so overwhelmed that she struggles to make even small decisions.

This persistent feeling of being overwhelmed, of having to work "10 times harder than others to complete simple tasks" , and the constant fear of being seen as "incapable" contributes to a profound sense of inadequacy.

This guide is designed to address this complex, interconnected reality. By providing a holistic approach that validates the lived experience of women with ADHD, it aims to empower them to move beyond a lifetime of self-blame and shame. The following books will provide evidence-based strategies to address the five core pillars of living a balanced and fulfilling life with ADHD. By providing a comprehensive roadmap, it aims to empower women to not just manage their symptoms but to truly thrive, transforming their unique neurobiology into a source of strength.

BOOK ONE:

ORGANIZE YOUR LIFE:

AN EASY GUIDE FOR WOMEN WITH ADHD

INTRODUCTION:

THE COGNITIVE COST OF DISORGANIZATION

For women with ADHD, organization is not a simple matter of tidiness or a character trait; it is a profound struggle that drains mental energy and fuels a persistent sense of overwhelm. The inability to maintain order in one's physical and digital environments is a direct symptom of the disorder, a consequence of inherent difficulties with executive functions like working memory, planning, and task initiation.

This chronic disorganization is not merely inconvenient; it carries a significant cognitive and emotional cost. Valuable time is lost in frantic searches for misplaced items, crucial opportunities are missed due to forgotten deadlines or buried documents, and the constant visual and mental clutter creates a pervasive background hum of anxiety. This struggle is often compounded by societal expectations for women to be the caretakers of an organized home, leading to a deep sense of shame that can manifest in painful ways, such as avoiding having people over due to the mess.

Therefore, this guide approaches organization not as a rigid, perfectionistic ideal, but as a form of self-care. The goal is to establish "functional organization," a system that reduces cognitive load, minimizes friction, and works for the unique wiring of the ADHD brain, rather than against it.

For many women, the struggle with disorganization is a relentless and often invisible battle. Research indicates that executive function (EF) skills, which are essential for managing daily tasks and responsibilities, are significantly challenged in adults with ADHD. These deficits can lead to difficulty staying focused, disorganization, and missed details, all of which directly contribute to a messy physical and digital environment.

For instance, a woman with ADHD might find herself wasting time looking for everyday items, with her home being so cluttered that she dislikes having people over. The symptoms that define ADHD, such as inattention, can manifest as a disorganized workstation, poor time management, and an inability to work in noisy or busy environments.

This chronic disorganization creates a constant, low-grade stress that permeates daily life. The mind, much like the physical space it inhabits, is cluttered, making it difficult to find mental clarity. The brain's working memory, which functions as a "mental scratchpad," can feel like a sieve, making it nearly impossible to remember where an item was placed just moments ago or to hold a multi-step organizational plan in mind.

It's a challenge so common that it's often described as the "out of sight, out of mind" phenomenon, where if something is put away in an opaque container or a cluttered drawer, it ceases to exist for the ADHD brain.

This struggle with disorganization is not a personal failing; it is a direct result of a neurobiological difference. For the ADHD brain, the very act of trying to start an organizing task can trigger a feeling of paralysis, a "can't get started" syndrome often referred to as a deficit in "task activation". The sheer scope of organizing a messy room or cleaning a cluttered inbox can trigger a feeling of overwhelm that makes task initiation nearly impossible.

The solution, as this guide will explore, is to break down these overwhelming tasks into smaller, more manageable steps. For example, instead of "Organize the entire bedroom," a more approachable task might be "Make the bed and place dirty clothes in the hamper". This systematic breakdown reduces the cognitive load and makes the first step feel psychologically approachable, transforming a daunting project into a series of achievable, low-friction steps.

The emotional toll of this disorganization is profound and often underestimated. Living with chronic disorganization and the constant effort to manage its consequences can lead to low self-esteem, self-blame, and feelings of inadequacy. Many women with undiagnosed ADHD endure childhoods filled with misunderstanding and self-blame, with a deep-seated feeling that there is something personally wrong with them.

Without a diagnosis, they may lack a better explanation for their struggles, attributing their challenges to personal flaws and developing a negative self-image. These women may also experience shame and frustration when they compare themselves to their peers and feel they are not living up to societal expectations. This constant inner critic and a repeated pattern of frustrations due to ADHD can contribute to or worsen co-occurring conditions like anxiety and depression.

This emotional burden is compounded by pervasive societal gender norms and roles. Society has long held the expectation for women to "do it all": to excel in both their public and private lives. While women have increasingly entered the workforce, they are still expected to shoulder the majority of household and domestic work.

It creates a "double burden" where women are under pressure to be perfect multitaskers, managing careers, households, and social lives simultaneously. Disorganization and messiness are often seen as violations of these traditional feminine norms, making women with ADHD particularly vulnerable to social judgment and internalizing feelings of inadequacy. When a woman with ADHD struggles to maintain an organized home, she may feel a deep sense of shame because her symptoms conflict with the unrealistic standards imposed on her.

This pressure can lead to feelings of overwhelm, anxiety, and a sense of inadequacy when they inevitably fail to meet these impossible standards. This guide rejects the notion of a rigid, perfectionistic ideal. Instead, it champions a more compassionate and strategic approach to organization.

The goal is to establish "functional organization," a system that is intentionally designed to work with the unique wiring of the ADHD brain rather than against it. Functional organization is not about a perfect, magazine-ready home, but about creating external systems that reduce cognitive load, minimize friction, and create predictability. This includes using visual cues like clear storage bins and labels to combat the "out of sight, out of mind" problem and giving every item a designated "home" to eliminate constant decision-making about where to put things away.

It also involves adopting digital systems, such as a planner that is checked multiple times a day, to externalize crucial information and combat working memory issues. The foundation of this approach is self-compassion, acknowledging that a woman's struggle with organization is a neurobiological reality, not a personal failing. It is about building a supportive environment that frees up mental energy, which can then be redirected towards more fulfilling and productive endeavors.

By mastering these foundational systems, a woman can create a stable and predictable base for the more complex skills of focus, emotion management, and relationship nurturing that will be explored in the following books. A truly organized external life creates a sense of calm and clarity that allows the internal chaos to subside, paving the way for sustained growth and well-being.

CHAPTER 1:

UNDERSTANDING THE ORGANIZATIONAL BRAIN

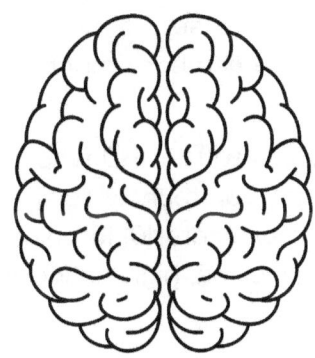

A foundational understanding of how the ADHD brain operates is essential to building an effective organizational system. The challenges with organization and planning are not a result of laziness or a lack of motivation; they are rooted in specific executive function differences.

Executive dysfunction is a range of behavioral symptoms that affect how a person regulates their emotions, thoughts, and actions, and it is a key symptom of ADHD. In fact, research indicates that the parts of the brain responsible for executive functions tend to be smaller, less developed, or less active in people with ADHD, which is why the disorder is nearly always associated with these symptoms.

Working memory, the brain's "mental scratchpad," can feel like a sieve, making it difficult to remember where an item was placed just moments ago or to hold a multi-step organizational plan in mind. Without a robust internal system for managing tasks and information, it is easy to become overwhelmed by the sheer number of things that need to be done.

The very act of trying to start an organizing task can trigger a feeling of paralysis, leading to procrastination. This is why a new approach is needed, one that validates the struggle and offers a compassionate, strategic way forward. The approach here is to externalize the cognitive load by building physical and digital structures that compensate for internal inconsistencies.

The Neurobiology of Executive Function Deficits

The organizational brain for a woman with ADHD operates on a different, and often more demanding, set of rules. Executive function (EF) is not a single skill, but a set of mental processes that allow a person to focus, plan, remember important details, and control impulses.

For the 40-60% of adults with ADHD who experience significant EF deficits, these challenges profoundly disrupt their personal and professional lives. They often score 10-15 points lower on EF measures than those without the condition, highlighting a measurable difference in cognitive ability.

This is not a matter of willpower, but rather a direct result of how the brain is wired. Research on memory and ADHD has found that these challenges are likely due to differences in the activation of various parts of the brain, including a reduced activation in the prefrontal cortex and cerebellum.

The prefrontal cortex is the brain's "command center" and is responsible for a variety of higher-level cognitive functions, such as planning, working memory, and impulse control. This reduced activity makes it more challenging to remember task goals, instructions, or rules. For example, the ADHD brain may process information in a disorganized manner, making it difficult to successfully move new information from short-term to long-term memory. This means that while the core machinery for memory is present, the process of encoding and retrieving information is often impaired.

This deficit can manifest as "brain fog," a temporary sluggishness and slowdown of your thinking abilities, leading to mental exhaustion, poor focus, carelessness, and forgetfulness. The cumulative effect of constantly fighting against this neurobiological reality is a profound sense of fatigue and being perpetually "frenzied, frazzled, and overwhelmed".

The Concept of Cognitive Load

A key factor in understanding the organizational struggles of the ADHD brain is the concept of cognitive load. Cognitive load refers to the total amount of mental effort being used in working memory. For a neurotypical person, the brain is able to efficiently filter out irrelevant stimuli and prioritize information, thus managing the cognitive load effectively.

For an individual with ADHD, this filtering mechanism is often less efficient, causing the brain to take in and process a disproportionate amount of incoming information, both internal and external. A single open browser tab, an unread email, a stray object on a desk, or an intrusive thought can all compete for attention with the same intensity as the main task at hand.

Research indicates that a high cognitive load can have a disproportionately negative impact on performance for people with ADHD. Studies have shown that as cognitive load increases, individuals with ADHD experience reduced performance, greater reaction time variability, and reduced brain network efficiency compared to those without the condition. This means that a cluttered physical or digital space isn't just an inconvenience; it is a direct contributor to reduced cognitive function and task performance, as each piece of clutter represents a subtle, but persistent, demand on a brain already struggling to filter and prioritize.

This is why the phrase "out of sight, out of mind" is so prevalent for people with ADHD. The sheer cognitive burden of managing multiple opaque containers, a cluttered desk, or a chaotic calendar can lead to tasks, items, and appointments ceasing to exist for the ADHD brain once they are no longer in the immediate visual field. The result is a constant drain on mental energy and a pervasive feeling of being overwhelmed by even minor daily inconveniences.

The Task Activation Deficit

A foundational hurdle for many women with ADHD is the "task activation deficit," a difficulty in initiating tasks without excessive procrastination. You may know exactly what needs to be done, but the gap between intention and action can feel immense, like a vast chasm you can't cross. This isn't laziness, but a neurological hurdle rooted in the brain's reward and motivation system. The very act of trying to start an organizing task, especially one that is perceived as boring or overwhelming, can trigger a feeling of paralysis, leading to what some refer to as "ADHD paralysis".

This paralysis is often a direct result of the overwhelming nature of a multi-step task. For instance, a woman might know she needs to clean her room, but the thought of organizing toys, putting away clothes, and making her bed feels so daunting that she can't figure out where to start. The sheer volume of an undifferentiated task can trigger an immediate shutdown response, as the brain's executive functions struggle to find a clear entry point. This is why breaking a to-do down into smaller, more manageable chunks is a highly effective strategy for the ADHD brain. It reduces the cognitive load and makes the initial step psychologically approachable, transforming a formidable project into a series of small, achievable steps.

The challenge with organization is also exacerbated by other related executive function deficits, such as difficulties with planning, prioritizing, and time management. The ADHD brain may struggle to create a step-by-step plan to achieve a goal, or to sort out which tasks are most important and which can wait. This combination of challenges makes it difficult to even begin the process of getting organized, creating a vicious cycle of disorganization leading to overwhelm, which in turn leads to procrastination.

The Emotional and Social Toll

This constant, daily struggle with organization and executive function deficits takes a significant emotional toll on women with ADHD, who often internalize their difficulties and blame themselves for their struggles. Research suggests that women with undiagnosed ADHD often endure childhoods filled with misunderstanding, self-blame, and rejection, with a persistent feeling that there is something personally wrong with them.

Without a clear explanation for their functional impairments, they may attribute their struggles to personal flaws, resulting in low self-esteem, shame, and a negative self-image. One woman with undiagnosed ADHD reported feeling "what I felt was I was actually a bad person... I was not an adequate human being".

This inner critic is often amplified by societal expectations for women to be the caretakers of an organized home and to perform as perfect multitaskers. When a woman with ADHD struggles to maintain order, her symptoms conflict with these unrealistic gender norms, leading to a profound sense of shame that can manifest in painful ways, such as avoiding having people over due to the mess. This constant pressure to meet impossible standards can lead to mental health struggles, including anxiety, depression, and feelings of inadequacy.

The emotional distress that arises from these challenges can be so severe that it contributes to or worsens co-occurring conditions, and it can be a source of significant distress and self-loathing.

Therefore, this guide approaches organization not as a rigid, perfectionistic ideal, but as a form of self-care. The goal is to establish "functional organization," a system that reduces cognitive load, minimizes friction, and works for the unique wiring of the ADHD brain, rather than against it. This compassionate, strategic approach is designed to free a woman from the debilitating cycle of self-blame and overwhelm, allowing her to build external systems that compensate for internal inconsistencies and create a sense of calm and clarity in her life. It is about understanding that your brain is not broken; it is simply wired differently and requires a tailored approach to thrive.

CHAPTER 2:

CREATING INTUITIVE PHYSICAL SYSTEMS

Your physical environment can be either a source of stress or a powerful ally in your pursuit of a more organized life. The first step in creating a supportive space is to recognize the common challenge known as "out of sight, out of mind". For an ADHD brain, if something is tucked away in an opaque container or a cluttered drawer, it ceases to exist. This can be directly combated by using clear storage bins and labels to keep everything visible and easily identifiable. The key is to create intuitive systems that minimize the mental effort required to maintain them.

A foundational principle is to give every single item a designated "home". By assigning a specific place for everything, you eliminate the constant decision-making about where to put something away, a process that drains executive function and leads to clutter. For frequently lost items, such as keys, wallets, and phones, the use of a "landing strip" near the front door is a highly effective strategy that ensures these crucial items are always in a predictable and easily accessible location.

To manage the inevitable accumulation of new items, consider implementing a "one-in, one-out" rule, which forces a conscious decision and prevents your home from becoming overwhelmed.

Maintaining these systems does not require constant, perfectionistic tidying. For the ADHD brain, a more sustainable approach is to schedule regular "resets" or "start-of-day/end-of-day clean-ups". These short, dedicated periods allow you to put things back in their homes and prevent small messes from spiraling into overwhelming chaos. This approach transforms organization from a source of frustration into a manageable, routine practice.

The Emotional and Cognitive Cost of Clutter

The relationship between your physical environment and your brain is a two-way street. For a neurotypical individual, a cluttered space might be a minor inconvenience, but for a woman with ADHD, it can be a significant source of cognitive and emotional distress. Research has consistently shown that cluttered environments can increase stress and anxiety and reduce productivity. A study in the *Personality and Social Psychology Bulletin* found that cluttered spaces can raise cortisol levels, which is a stress hormone that can exacerbate ADHD symptoms.

This constant, low-grade stress is not just a feeling; it is a measurable cognitive drain. Each item in a cluttered space represents a potential point of distraction, demanding a fraction of your attention and consuming valuable working memory and executive function resources. Your brain, already working harder to filter out irrelevant stimuli, becomes overloaded by the sheer volume of visual and sensory information.

The result is a pervasive background hum of anxiety, mental exhaustion, and a feeling of being overwhelmed that can lead to procrastination and a complete shutdown, or what is often referred to as "ADHD paralysis."

This struggle is often compounded by powerful societal expectations for women to be the caretakers of an organized home. When a woman with ADHD struggles to maintain order, her symptoms conflict with these unrealistic gender norms, leading to a profound sense of shame that can manifest in painful ways, such as avoiding having people over due to the mess.

Research shows that women with undiagnosed ADHD often endure childhoods filled with misunderstanding, self-blame, and a persistent feeling that there is something personally wrong with them, a feeling that is exacerbated by the internal and external pressures related to organization.

The "Out of Sight, Out of Mind" Phenomenon: A Deeper Look

The idea that "if something is out of sight, it's out of mind" is a widely recognized experience for people with ADHD and is directly tied to challenges with working memory. Working memory is the brain's "mental scratchpad," and for a woman with ADHD, that scratchpad can feel like a sieve, making it difficult to hold information in mind for a short period of time.

As a result, if an item is not in your immediate visual field, your brain may fail to register its existence, location, or importance, leading to frantic searches for misplaced items and a constant feeling of being disorganized.

This is why traditional organizational advice, such as "tuck everything away neatly in opaque boxes," can be completely counterproductive for the ADHD brain. Instead of creating a sense of order, it creates a system of unreliability where items are lost the moment they are hidden. To counteract this, the organizational system must be intentionally designed to be visual and to externalize the cognitive load. By making everything visible and easily identifiable, you bypass the need for your working memory to constantly recall where an item is, allowing you to use that precious mental energy for other, more demanding tasks.

Strategies to combat this challenge include:

- **Clear Storage Bins:** Using clear bins or containers allows you to see the contents without having to open them, providing a constant visual cue of what is inside. This is a simple but powerful way to ensure that your items remain "in mind."

- **Labels, Labels, Labels:** For items that must be stored in opaque containers or drawers, clear, bold labels are essential. A label for "Office Supplies" or "First Aid Kit" serves as a crucial external reminder of the contents, eliminating the mental effort of guessing or having to search through every drawer.

- **Vertical Organization:** Piles of papers or objects on a flat surface can be a source of overwhelm and mental friction. Using clipboards to display current projects as a visual reminder or vertical file folders to keep important paperwork in sight can help manage this. This approach transforms an overwhelming pile into a manageable, visual system of organization.

The Power of a Designated "Home"

A foundational principle of intuitive physical systems is to give every single item a designated "home". This is not about being rigid or a perfectionist; it is a strategic approach to reduce decision fatigue, which is a major drain on executive function. Each time you pick up an item, your brain is faced with a micro-decision: "Where does this go?" When you don't have a clear, pre-determined "home" for an item, that micro-decision process can lead to an endless loop of deliberation that often ends with the item being placed on a random surface, contributing to clutter and chaos.

By assigning a specific and predictable place for every item, you eliminate this decision-making process. Putting an item away becomes a simple, automatic, and low-friction action. For frequently lost items, such as keys, wallets, phones, and glasses, a "landing strip" near the front door or a designated bowl on a counter is a highly effective, research-backed strategy that ensures these crucial items are always in a predictable and easily accessible location. By creating a system of predictability, you free up your mental resources and reduce the frantic, time-consuming searches that so often accompany ADHD.

This principle extends to all areas of your life, from the keys on the landing strip to the remote control on the coffee table to the notebooks on your desk. By making the "home" for an item obvious and intuitive, you build a system that works with your brain's unique wiring, not against it.

Maintenance Made Manageable: The Role of Routines

For the ADHD brain, the idea of "constant tidying" can feel like an impossible and overwhelming ideal that is destined for failure. This is why a perfectionistic approach to organization is often a fast track to burnout and abandonment of the system altogether. A more sustainable approach is to create and implement simple, non-negotiable routines and maintenance rituals.

One of the most effective strategies is to schedule regular "resets" or "start-of-day/end-of-day clean-ups". This involves dedicating a short, consistent period of time, for instance, 15 minutes in the morning or evening, to tidying up your physical and digital workspaces. This prevents small messes from snowballing into overwhelming mountains of clutter that seem impossible to tackle. The goal is not a pristine space, but a functional one. For example, instead of trying to keep an entire bedroom clean all the time, you could commit to simply making your bed and placing dirty clothes in a hamper at the start of each day. This small, manageable commitment provides a sense of accomplishment and prevents a small mess from spiraling into overwhelming chaos.

The "one-in, one-out" rule also plays a vital role in maintaining the system over time. This simple principle is a powerful preventative measure against the inevitable accumulation of new items that can quickly overwhelm a space. By forcing a conscious decision to remove an item every time a new one is introduced, you actively prevent your home from becoming a source of cognitive and physical clutter.

These maintenance routines are crucial because they transform organization from a source of frustration and anxiety into a manageable, routine practice that is integrated into your daily life. It acknowledges the reality that things will get messy and builds in a compassionate, strategic way to address it without succumbing to overwhelm or self-criticism.

Conclusion: Your External Sanctuary

This chapter has provided a roadmap for creating a physical environment that is not just organized, but is a sanctuary for your ADHD brain. By understanding the profound cognitive and emotional costs of disorganization, a woman can move beyond self-blame and begin to work with her brain, not against it. She has learned to combat the "out of sight, out of mind" phenomenon with visual cues and clear labels, to give every item a "home" to reduce decision fatigue, and to maintain her systems with realistic, non-perfectionistic routines.

The mastery of these strategies transforms your physical space from a source of friction and stress into a powerful ally for focus, clarity, and peace. It frees up immense mental energy that was once consumed by searching for misplaced items, navigating clutter, and feeling overwhelmed.

This newly available cognitive bandwidth can then be redirected toward more fulfilling and productive endeavors. A truly organized external life creates a sense of calm and clarity that allows the internal chaos to subside, paving the way for sustained growth and well-being.

CHAPTER 3:

TAMING THE DIGITAL DELUGE

In the modern world, the digital realm can be an even greater source of disorganization and overwhelm than the physical one. A chaotic email inbox, a cluttered computer desktop, and a scattered collection of digital notes can all contribute to mental friction and a sense of being perpetually behind. The goal here is to establish simple, intuitive systems that minimize the cognitive burden of digital management.

For the ADHD brain, the digital world is a double-edged sword. On one hand, it offers a wealth of tools and external reminders that can be invaluable for compensating for working memory deficits. A digital planner with automatic alerts can provide the crucial structure needed to remember appointments and deadlines.

On the other hand, the digital environment is a hyper-stimulating landscape of endless distractions, notifications, and open loops that are perfectly designed to hijack an already scattered attention span. A single open browser tab can be a subtle demand on your attention, a pending notification can trigger an impulsive check, and a cluttered desktop can create a visual and cognitive drain that is as potent as a messy physical space.

This relentless barrage of digital stimuli exacerbates the struggle with executive functions like working memory and attention regulation, leading to what research refers to as high "cognitive load". Studies have shown that for individuals with ADHD, increasing cognitive load disproportionately reduces performance, increases reaction time variability, and decreases brain network efficiency compared to those without the condition . Therefore, just as you learned to intentionally design your physical space, mastering your digital environment is a non-negotiable step toward a more organized and peaceful life.

The Email Onslaught: Taming the Inbox

The email inbox is often a primary source of digital overwhelm, quickly transforming from a communication tool into a chaotic, constantly-updating to-do list that triggers a persistent sense of anxiety and defeat. The constant stream of messages demands attention and decision-making, a process that is particularly draining for the ADHD brain.

An effective strategy is to implement a triage system that reduces the cognitive load and turns email management into a predictable, low-friction process.

A core strategy for email is the "Inbox Zero" concept, but viewed through the lens of a clear, actionable system rather than a stressful ideal. This involves a four-step triage process for every email: delete it if it's junk, do it if it takes less than two minutes, delegate it to someone else, or defer it by moving it to a specific "To Do" folder in your email client.

By consistently processing your inbox this way, you prevent it from becoming a cluttered to-do list that drains your attention and provides a sense of overwhelming defeat. This process is not about achieving an empty inbox at all costs, but about consciously deciding the fate of each email and preventing the mental clutter that comes from having an open-ended list of pending tasks.

The "two-minute rule" is especially powerful for the ADHD brain because it leverages the psychological power of quick wins. By immediately tackling small, manageable tasks, you get a satisfying hit of dopamine, which reinforces productive behavior and builds momentum for the more demanding tasks that require a deferred response. This triage system also externalizes decision-making, so your brain is no longer constantly asking, "What should I do with this?"

This intentional processing reduces the mental friction of an unmanaged inbox and creates a sense of control over a traditionally chaotic digital space.

For managing the inflow of emails, consider creating dedicated email blocks in your daily schedule. Instead of leaving your email client open all day and reacting to each incoming message, which constantly fragments your attention, dedicate two or three specific 20-minute periods to process your inbox. This practice turns email from a persistent distraction into a manageable, time-bound task.

You can also create simple rules or filters to automatically send newsletters, notifications, or less important messages to a designated folder, ensuring that your main inbox remains a clear space for high-priority communication.

The Digital Planner: Your External Working Memory

For a woman with ADHD, relying solely on internal working memory to keep track of deadlines, appointments, and tasks is a recipe for anxiety and forgetfulness. As research has shown, working memory deficits are a core feature of the disorder, and these challenges are linked to a reduced activation in the prefrontal cortex, which is the brain's command center for planning and memory. This is why externalizing your memory is a crucial compensatory strategy.

The use of a simple, digital planner is also crucial for combating the working memory issues inherent in ADHD by externalizing important deadlines and tasks. By checking this planner at least twice a day, once in the morning and once at night, a woman can eliminate the fear of forgetting a crucial deadline or appointment. Digital planners, calendars, and apps with reminders and alerts are particularly effective because they provide a reliable, automated system that doesn't rely on inconsistent internal memory.

When setting up your digital planner, be intentional:

- **Color-Code:** Use a color-coding system to visually represent different areas of your life, such as work, personal appointments, family events, and self-care. Visual cues make your schedule easier for the ADHD brain to process and understand at a glance.
- **Time Block:** Don't just list tasks; block out specific time slots for them. Time blocking helps make time more tangible by assigning a finite duration to a task, which is a powerful antidote to "time blindness".
- **Set Multiple Reminders:** For important deadlines or appointments, set multiple alarms or alerts. Set one for a week before, one for a day before, and one for an hour before. This redundancy provides crucial support for a brain that can easily be derailed by last-minute distractions.

By consistently relying on an external planner, you offload the immense cognitive burden of remembering everything, freeing up your mental energy for focused work and creative thinking.

Digital Filing: The "Less is More" Approach

A cluttered digital workspace—a desktop covered in files, a downloads folder with hundreds of unsorted documents, and a complex hierarchy of folders—is a significant drain on cognitive resources. The ADHD brain, already struggling to filter out irrelevant information, can become quickly overwhelmed by digital disorganization. The mental effort required to navigate a chaotic digital environment, remember where files are, and make decisions about where to save new documents creates unnecessary mental friction.

To combat this, the most effective strategy is to adopt a "less is more" approach to digital filing by creating a few broad, consistently used folders and relying on powerful search functions. This approach is not about a rigid, perfectionistic system but about creating a simple, intuitive structure that is easy to maintain.

- **Create a Flat Hierarchy:** Instead of creating a deeply nested folder structure (e.g., Documents > Work > Client A > Project X > Research > Q1), create a flat hierarchy with a few main folders that are easy to navigate (e.g., Projects, Clients, Reference, Archive). The ADHD brain can easily get lost in a complex folder structure.

- **Use Consistent Naming Conventions:** Implement a simple naming convention for your files (e.g., ProjectName_DocumentType_Date). This makes it easier to find files using the search bar, which should be your primary tool for locating information.

- **Leverage Search:** Modern operating systems and cloud storage platforms have incredibly powerful search functions. By relying on a consistent naming system, you can use search as your main tool for finding documents, eliminating the need to remember complex folder paths. This is an external solution that bypasses your working memory deficits.

- **Desktop Decluttering:** Treat your computer desktop as a temporary holding space, not a permanent storage solution. Move all files from your desktop to a single, designated "To Sort" folder at the end of each day or week. This prevents visual clutter from accumulating and reduces the cognitive load of a messy digital space.

Taming Digital Noise and Distractions

The digital world is a constant source of interruptions that can derail focus and fragment attention for the ADHD brain. Each notification, pop-up, or email chime is a "ping" that pulls your mental spotlight away from your current task. The brain's tendency to struggle with filtering out irrelevant stimuli means that these digital pings are given disproportionate weight, making it incredibly difficult to achieve a state of "deep work."

A powerful strategy is to create a digital "attention zone" by proactively minimizing distractions:

- **Notification Annihilation:** This is paramount. Turn off all non-essential notifications on your phone, tablet, and computer. Be ruthless. Turn off alerts for social media, news apps, and email clients. The fewer pings your devices make, the easier it is for your brain to stay on task.
- **App Management:** Regularly review the apps on your phone and computer. Delete those you don't use. For apps you find distracting, consider grouping them into a folder on your phone's last screen to create a deliberate moment of friction before you can access them.
- **Browser Management:** Commit to having only 1-3 tabs open at any given time. Each additional tab is an open loop that demands a piece of your working memory. Use browser extensions like "StayFocusd" or "Freedom" to block distracting websites during your work periods.
- **Digital Self-Care:** Recognize that digital clutter and noise are a source of stress. Schedule intentional periods of "digital detox" where you completely unplug from screens. This allows your brain to reset, reducing the mental fatigue that comes from constant digital stimulation.

By implementing these digital hygiene practices, you'll create a calmer, more focused digital environment that supports your attention rather than constantly fighting for it.

Leveraging Technology for Automation and Externalization

Beyond simple organization, modern technology offers powerful tools that can be leveraged to create automated systems that work for the ADHD brain, further reducing the need for conscious effort and decision-making.

- **Automate Everything:** Wherever possible, automate tasks that are repetitive or easy to forget. This is a highly effective way to combat the challenges of working memory and time blindness. Set up automatic bill payments, so you no longer have to worry about late fees. Use recurring calendar reminders for habits you want to build or tasks that need to be done regularly.

- **Use Visual Tools:** Many people with ADHD are visual thinkers. Use budgeting apps with charts and graphs, or project management tools with Kanban boards (like Trello) that allow you to see the entire flow of a project. These visual systems make abstract concepts more tangible and easier for the ADHD brain to process, reducing overwhelm and increasing task initiation.

- **Digital Backups:** Prevent the emotional distress and wasted time that comes with losing important files by regularly backing up your data. Use automated cloud backups or external hard drives. The emotional and cognitive cost of losing a critical document is immense, and this simple system provides a reliable safety net.

By embracing technology in these strategic ways, you're not just managing your digital life; you're building a sophisticated external support system that compensates for your internal challenges, allowing you to operate with greater efficiency, less stress, and more confidence.

Your Roadmap to Becoming Digital Savvy

This chapter has provided a roadmap for creating a digital environment that is not a source of constant stress and distraction, but a powerful ally in your pursuit of a more organized life. By understanding how digital clutter and noise contribute to cognitive overload for the ADHD brain, you can move beyond a reactive, frantic approach to a proactive, strategic one.

You have learned to:

- **Tame your email** with a low-friction triage system that reduces decision fatigue.
- **Externalize your working memory** with a digital planner that provides a reliable, visual anchor for your schedule and tasks.
- **Simplify your digital filing** with a "less is more" approach that leverages powerful search functions.
- **Build a digital sanctuary** by proactively managing notifications, browser tabs, and apps to protect your focus.

- **Leverage technology** for automation, visual support, and reliable backups that compensate for your internal challenges.

The mastery of these digital systems transforms your online world from a source of friction and overwhelm into a clean, intuitive, and supportive extension of your mind. This newly available cognitive bandwidth, once consumed by fighting digital chaos, can now be redirected towards more fulfilling and productive endeavors. A truly organized digital life creates a sense of calm and clarity that allows the internal chaos to subside, paving the way for sustained growth and well-being.

CHAPTER 4:

FROM IDEA TO ACTION:
SYSTEMS FOR CONSISTENT FOLLOW-THROUGH

A solid organizational system is invaluable, but it's only truly powerful when it bridges the gap between intention and action. The immense, amorphous nature of large projects can trigger a feeling of overwhelm that paralyzes the ADHD brain and makes task initiation nearly impossible. The solution to this is to systematically break down every large, intimidating task into smaller, more manageable chunks.

For example, instead of "Organize the Garage," a task could be broken down into "Clear one shelf" or "Sort tools into a basket." This reduces the cognitive burden and makes the first step feel psychologically approachable, transforming a daunting project into a series of achievable, low-friction steps.

The Chasm Between Intention and Action

For women with ADHD, the journey from a brilliant idea to a completed project is often fraught with a unique and frustrating barrier: the gap between intention and action. You may have a clear vision and a strong desire to accomplish a goal, but an invisible wall seems to prevent you from taking that crucial first step. This isn't a sign of laziness or a lack of motivation; it is a neurological hurdle, a symptom of a task activation deficit that is deeply intertwined with the brain's executive function challenges.

Research on the ADHD brain's executive functions, such as working memory, planning, and prioritization, has found that these skills are often less efficient, which can make getting started on tasks feel overwhelming, especially when there are multiple steps involved.

The sheer scale of a large, undifferentiated project, like "Write a business plan" or "Organize the entire closet", can trigger a state of mental paralysis known as "ADHD paralysis." For an ADHD brain, which already struggles with filtering and prioritizing, the cognitive load of holding a multi-step plan in mind can feel immense.

The brain's prefrontal cortex, which is responsible for these higher-level cognitive functions, can become overwhelmed, leading to a shutdown response rather than initiation. The solution, therefore, is not to simply "try harder," but to create a strategic and compassionate system that bypasses this internal resistance by externalizing the cognitive load and making the initial step so small and non-intimidating that the activation energy required is minimal.

The Art and Science of Task Breakdown

The core strategy for bridging the gap between intention and action is to systematically break down every large, intimidating task into smaller, more manageable chunks. This process reduces cognitive overwhelm and makes the first step feel psychologically approachable, transforming a daunting project into a series of achievable, low-friction steps.

Research indicates that breaking tasks into smaller chunks reduces cognitive load and increases task initiation, which is crucial for a brain that struggles with executive function deficits.

This is not a purely theoretical exercise; it is a practical art with a scientific basis. The ADHD brain is constantly seeking a fresh hit of dopamine, the neurotransmitter associated with motivation and reward. By breaking down a large task into smaller steps, you create more opportunities for a sense of accomplishment and a satisfying burst of dopamine each time you complete one. This positive reinforcement loop builds momentum, making it easier to sustain your effort over time.

Here's how to apply a systematic approach to task breakdown:

- **The Brain Dump:** Before you can organize a project, you must first get everything out of your head. Write down every single thought, step, worry, and idea related to the large task onto a piece of paper, a whiteboard, or a digital note-taking app. Don't worry about order or logic; just get it all out. This externalizes the mental clutter and provides a raw inventory of the project, freeing up your working memory for a more organized approach.

- **Identify the "Next Action":** For every item on your list, ask yourself: "What is the very next physical action I need to take to move this forward?" The key is to make this step so small that it feels almost ridiculous not to do it. Instead of "Clean the kitchen," the next action might be "Put one dish in the dishwasher." Instead of "Write the report," it could be "Open a new document and type the title." This micro-commitment lowers the activation energy required to begin, making procrastination less likely.

- **Create a Visual Checklist:** Once you have a series of tiny, actionable steps, transfer them to a visual checklist. This could be a physical list on a clipboard, a visual calendar with color-coded blocks, or a digital task manager like a Kanban board in Trello. The visual satisfaction of physically or digitally checking off small items provides valuable, immediate dopamine hits. This consistent, visible progress combats the feelings of stagnation and overwhelm that so often accompany large projects.

The Pomodoro Technique: A Structured Solution for Sustained Focus

The Pomodoro Technique is an excellent tool to implement this strategy, as it breaks down the day into manageable, focused work sprints. It is particularly effective for the ADHD brain because it works

with its natural need for novelty and breaks, rather than fighting against it. The traditional technique involves committing to 25 minutes of uninterrupted, single-task focus, followed by a 5-minute break. After four of these cycles, you take a longer, more restorative break of 20-30 minutes.

The power of this technique for the ADHD brain lies in its built-in structure:

- **It Reduces Overwhelm:** The idea of working on a boring or difficult task for an undefined period can be paralyzing. Committing to a task for a short, manageable burst of 25 minutes makes it feel less intimidating and more approachable. This is a powerful antidote to "ADHD paralysis."

- **It Accommodates the Need for Breaks:** The scheduled 5-minute breaks provide regular, guilt-free opportunities for the brain to reset and seek novelty without derailing the entire work session. This prevents the mental fatigue and restlessness that can build up during prolonged, static focus. The breaks serve as a reward and a mental reset, accommodating the brain's natural rhythms.

- **It Builds Momentum:** The short, focused bursts help the ADHD brain get into a state of momentum. Once you're in motion, it's often easier to stay in motion. The consistent, rhythmic nature of the Pomodoro cycles helps to gradually train your brain to sustain attention for longer periods.

Research supports the efficacy of this approach. One study found that implementing the Pomodoro technique in a digital marketing company helped employees work more efficiently and improve their work-life balance. The discipline of single-tasking, enforced by a timer, is a powerful antidote to a scattered mind, allowing a woman to reduce feelings of overwhelm and achieve a higher quality of work with less mental effort.

Beyond Pomodoro: Additional Strategies for Consistent Follow-Through

While task breakdown and the Pomodoro Technique are foundational, there are other strategies that can be integrated to support consistent follow-through and counteract the ADHD brain's tendency to lose momentum.

- **Body Doubling:** Working alongside another person, either in person or virtually, can be a remarkably effective way to combat "activation energy" deficits and sustain focus. The mere presence of another person provides a subtle sense of accountability and structure, making it easier to start and remain on task without relying solely on willpower. The other person acts as an external executive function, providing a stable, non-distracting presence that helps anchor your attention.

- **Gamification and Rewards:** The ADHD brain thrives on immediate feedback and rewards. To maintain momentum on a long task, inject elements of a game into your work. Use a timer to "compete" against yourself, create a points system for completed sub-tasks, or build in small, intentional rewards for hitting a milestone. The promise of an immediate, enjoyable reward, like a 5-minute break, a favorite song, or a cup of tea, can provide the necessary dopamine hit to push through a tedious section of a project.

- **The "One-in, One-out" Rule (for Tasks):** Just as you might apply this rule to physical items to prevent clutter, you can apply it to your to-do list. Commit to finishing one task before you allow yourself to start a new one. This prevents the "half-finished pile" from accumulating and forces you to bring tasks to completion. It's a deliberate act of single-tasking that builds a habit of follow-through.

- **Embrace Imperfection:** For many women with ADHD, perfectionism is a subtle but powerful form of procrastination. The fear of not doing something perfectly can prevent you from starting or, more commonly, from finishing. Remind yourself constantly that "done is better than perfect." The goal is completion and tangible progress, not flawlessness. A completed, even imperfect, project creates momentum and allows for iteration, while a "perfect" project that is perpetually stuck in the planning stage serves no one.

- **Public Accountability:** Tell a trusted friend, partner, or colleague what specific task you intend to accomplish by a certain time. Knowing someone else is aware of your commitment can provide a powerful external motivator to follow through, leveraging social pressure to push past resistance. This can be as simple as a quick text: "I'm going to finish the draft of that report by 3 PM."

This intentional, systematic approach to task management is fundamental to converting intentions into tangible accomplishments. By understanding the neurobiological hurdles of task initiation and follow-through, and by consistently implementing these evidence-based strategies, a woman can transform her relationship with productivity. She learns to build a bridge across the chasm of procrastination, creating a clear and reliable path from a brilliant idea to a tangible, satisfying reality.

CHAPTER 5:

THE ORGANIZED MIND:
HABIT BUILDING AND MAINTENANCE

Building a functional organizational system is not a one-time event; it is an ongoing practice that requires building and maintaining habits. The ADHD brain can find it particularly challenging to maintain organization consistently, but this can be addressed by implementing structured routines. A powerful strategy is to conduct regular "resets" or "start-of-day/end-of-day clean-ups".

This involves dedicating a short, consistent period of time, for instance, 15 minutes in the morning or evening, to tidying up your physical and digital workspaces. This prevents small messes from snowballing into overwhelming mountains of clutter that seem impossible to tackle.

Additionally, a key to maintaining momentum is to tackle small, manageable parts of a larger task. This approach provides frequent, small wins and a tangible sense of progress that fuels continued effort. For example, instead of committing to "Clean the entire kitchen," one could simply focus on "Washing the dishes".

This reduces the sense of being overwhelmed and provides a feeling of accomplishment that makes it easier to continue the work later. The ultimate goal is to create a rhythm of organization that becomes an intuitive, supportive part of your daily routine, rather than a frustrating chore.

The Neurobiology of Habit Formation in the ADHD Brain

For a woman with ADHD, the process of building and maintaining a habit can feel like trying to build a sandcastle against a relentless tide. While the intention is there, the follow-through often falters. This isn't a failure of willpower, but a direct result of how the ADHD brain's reward system and executive functions operate.

Habits are typically formed through a cycle of cue, routine, and reward, but for a brain with dysregulated dopamine, the reward from a mundane, long-term habit can feel too distant or too small to motivate consistent action. The brain craves immediate, satisfying hits of dopamine, which are often not provided by the repetitive, unglamorous tasks required to maintain organization.

Furthermore, the executive function deficits that make organization so difficult in the first place, such as challenges with working memory, task initiation, and prioritization, also make habit formation a significant hurdle. A woman might forget the steps of a new routine, find it impossible to start the habit without an external cue, or feel so overwhelmed by the sheer number of things to remember that the routine is abandoned before it even begins. This is why a traditional, rigid approach to habit formation is often counterproductive.

The key to success is to build a system that works with the ADHD brain's wiring, leveraging its need for novelty, external cues, and immediate rewards to make maintenance feel less like a chore and more like a game.

Creating a Routine-Based Framework for Maintenance

Instead of aiming for constant, perfectionistic tidiness, a more sustainable approach is to implement flexible, structured routines that provide stability without feeling restrictive. These routines reduce decision fatigue, a common challenge for the ADHD brain, by creating predictable pathways for action that don't require conscious thought or a sudden burst of motivation. Research from

Cognitive Development has shown that predictable environments can improve cognitive functioning, which is precisely what these routines aim to create.

A powerful strategy is to conduct regular "resets" or "start-of-day/end-of-day clean-ups". These aren't meant to be exhaustive deep cleans, but rather short, dedicated periods to tidy up and put things back in their designated homes. This prevents small messes from snowballing into overwhelming mountains of clutter that seem impossible to tackle, a state that often triggers "ADHD paralysis" or procrastination.

- **The End-of-Day Reset:** Dedicate 10-15 minutes at the end of each day to a quick reset of your physical and digital workspaces. This could involve putting away dishes, clearing a specific surface, or processing your email inbox. The purpose is to close out the day with a sense of order and to prevent tomorrow's self from being overwhelmed by today's mess.

- **The Start-of-Day Clean-Up:** Similarly, spend a few minutes each morning to tidy up. For many, simply making the bed and placing dirty clothes in a hamper can create a sense of order and accomplishment that sets a positive tone for the entire day. This micro-commitment lowers the activation energy required to engage with the day's tasks, which is a major hurdle for the ADHD brain.

- **The Weekly Review:** In addition to daily resets, schedule a 30-minute weekly review session to declutter a specific area and get back on track. This could be processing all the mail that has piled up, tackling a messy drawer, or organizing a downloads folder. This dedicated, time-bound session prevents a general sense of chaos from accumulating and provides a fresh slate for the week ahead.

The Power of Small, Actionable Steps: The "Swiss Cheese" Method

Habit maintenance for a woman with ADHD often fails when a task feels too large or overwhelming. This is where the concept of breaking down tasks into small, manageable parts becomes a crucial, continuous strategy. This approach provides frequent, small wins and a tangible sense of progress that fuels continued effort. Research from

Neuropsychology Review confirms that breaking down tasks into smaller chunks reduces cognitive load and increases task initiation, both of which are core challenges for the ADHD brain.

The "Swiss Cheese" method is a useful metaphor for this approach. Instead of trying to tackle a solid block of a large, intimidating task, you simply "poke holes" in it by committing to completing a small, manageable part of it. For example, instead of committing to "Clean the entire kitchen," one could simply focus on "Washing the dishes" or "Wiping down the counters".

This reduces the sense of being overwhelmed and provides a feeling of accomplishment that makes it easier to continue the work later. The immediate, satisfying feeling of a completed micro-task provides a much-needed burst of dopamine that reinforces productive behavior and builds momentum for the next step. This strategy transforms a seemingly insurmountable task into a series of achievable, low-friction steps, and is particularly effective at overcoming the "all-or-nothing" thinking that often leads to procrastination and avoidance.

Leveraging Motivation and Positive Reinforcement

For the ADHD brain, motivation is often a product of immediate reward rather than a sense of long-term accomplishment. Therefore, a successful maintenance system must be intentionally designed with positive reinforcement in mind. After all, if the behavior isn't rewarding, the brain is far less likely to repeat it.

- **Gamify the Task:** Making an organizational task feel like a game can be an excellent way to boost motivation. Set a timer and see if you can beat your previous time. Give yourself points for each item you put away. The element of competition or play can provide the necessary stimulation to get through a boring or repetitive task.

- **Pair the Task with a Reward:** Intentionally pair a dreaded chore with something you genuinely enjoy. For example, "I will only listen to my favorite podcast while I'm doing the laundry," or "I'll allow myself to have a cup of tea and read a chapter of my book once the dishes are done." This strategy is a form of "temptation bundling," which makes the unpleasant task feel more palatable by linking it to an immediate, positive reward.

- **Focus on the "Now" and Celebrate the Win:** A woman with ADHD may experience a strong emotional response to the perception of failure or disapproval. To counteract this, it's crucial to focus on the present moment and the small, tangible wins of each day. Instead of dwelling on past mistakes or times when you felt disorganized, celebrate your successful efforts. The simple act of checking a task off a list or admiring a clean counter can provide a powerful sense of accomplishment that fuels continued effort.

The Organized Mind: A Continuous Cycle of Review and Adaptation

Ultimately, the goal is to create a rhythm of organization that becomes an intuitive, supportive part of your daily routine, rather than a frustrating chore. This process is not a linear journey, and there will be days when routines are missed, tasks are forgotten, and chaos creeps back in. The key to sustainable maintenance is not rigid adherence to a perfect system, but rather a compassionate, iterative process of review and adaptation.

Instead of engaging in harsh self-criticism when a system fails, a woman can use these moments as a form of valuable data collection. She can ask herself: "What happened here? What was the friction point? What made this system hard to maintain today?"

By approaching these moments with curiosity and compassion, she can learn from them and make small, strategic adjustments to her systems, making them more resilient and effective over time. This continuous cycle of review, adaptation, and refinement is the true foundation of a well-organized and peaceful life. It's about building a supportive, forgiving relationship with your brain, and creating a system that is as flexible and dynamic as your unique neurobiology requires.

Conclusion: Your Foundational Systems

This book has provided a blueprint for building foundational systems for organization. The core of this work has been about externalizing the burdens of your ADHD brain, creating physical and digital structures that compensate for internal challenges with working memory, planning, and task initiation. By giving everything a home, simplifying your digital world, and breaking down overwhelming tasks into manageable steps, a woman can free up immense mental energy. This newly available cognitive bandwidth can then be redirected towards more fulfilling and productive endeavors.

The mastery of these foundational systems provides a stable and predictable base for the more complex skills of focus, emotion management, and relationship nurturing that will be explored in the following books. A truly organized external life creates a sense of calm and clarity that allows the internal chaos to subside, paving the way for sustained growth and well-being.

The Liberation of Externalizing the Mind

For many women with ADHD, the internal experience is one of a mind that is perpetually "frenzied, frazzled, and overwhelmed". This internal chaos is not an emotional state in isolation; it is a direct consequence of a brain that struggles with its core executive functions, such as working memory, planning, and prioritization.

Research shows that people with ADHD score significantly lower on executive function measures, highlighting a measurable difference in cognitive ability that is not related to intelligence. This neurobiological reality means that a woman's brain is constantly expending mental energy on tasks that neurotypical individuals do unconsciously, such as filtering out irrelevant stimuli or holding a multi-step plan in mind. This constant, conscious effort to manage internal inconsistencies creates a significant "ADHD tax," a measurable cognitive cost that leaves a woman mentally exhausted and with a diminished capacity for deep work or meaningful connection.

The strategies outlined in this book, such as giving every item a designated "home," using visual systems, and breaking down tasks, are all designed to externalize this immense cognitive burden. When a woman with ADHD can trust that her external systems (a planner, a calendar, a designated key hook) are reliable, she no longer has to use her inconsistent internal working memory to hold onto a mountain of information.

This act of offloading, of creating an "external brain," is profoundly liberating. It frees up immense mental bandwidth that was once consumed by the frantic, low-level anxiety of remembering where things are or what needs to be done. This is why a cluttered environment isn't just an inconvenience; it's a significant drain on executive function, as each piece of clutter represents a subtle demand on a brain already struggling to filter and prioritize. By consciously creating systems that work with the ADHD brain's wiring, a woman can transform her relationship with productivity from one of perpetual struggle to one of intentional action.

From Chaos to Calm: The Emotional Impact of Order

The impact of this foundational work on organization extends far beyond a tidy home or a clear inbox; it directly addresses the emotional toll that chronic disorganization takes on women with ADHD. For many, the constant struggle with organization is a source of profound shame, anxiety, and a shattered sense of self-worth. This struggle is often compounded by deeply ingrained societal expectations for women to be the caretakers of an organized and harmonious home. When a woman's ADHD symptoms, such as disorganization and messiness, violate these traditional feminine norms, she becomes particularly vulnerable to social judgment and feelings of inadequacy. Research shows that women with undiagnosed ADHD often endure childhoods filled with misunderstanding and self-blame, with a deep-seated feeling that they are "not an adequate human being" or that something is inherently "wrong" with them.

This cycle of shame, self-blame, and frustration is a direct contributor to co-occurring mental health conditions that are so prevalent in women with ADHD, such as anxiety and depression. The relentless pressure to perform, to "do it all," creates a "double burden" that leaves a woman feeling overwhelmed and undervalued . She might internalize her struggles and engage in the practice of "masking," where she develops sophisticated compensatory behaviors to hide her chaos and appear "neurotypical" to the outside world. This constant, exhausting effort to appear organized is an invisible burden that leads to a lifetime of internal shame and a sense of being an impostor.

By building a functional organizational system, a woman is not just tidying up her space; she is actively engaging in a powerful form of self-care. She is creating an external sanctuary that reduces the persistent background hum of anxiety and the internal chaos that so many women with ADHD report feeling. She is transforming her home from a source of stress into a supportive ally, a place where she no longer has to feel shame for the mess and can finally feel a sense of calm and clarity.

This mastery of her physical and digital worlds provides a tangible sense of control and self-efficacy, which is a powerful antidote to the feelings of helplessness and inadequacy that have so often accompanied her struggle with organization.

The Bridge to the Future: Paving the Way for Deeper Work

The work of organization is foundational because it is the prerequisite for all the more complex work that follows. A brain that is constantly consumed by the low-level noise of disorganization, the search for lost keys, the overwhelming email inbox, the mental energy spent on planning a simple task, is a brain that is unable to engage in the kind of deep work that is required for sustained focus, emotional regulation, and meaningful relationships.

The mastery of these foundational systems provides a stable and predictable base for the more complex skills of focus, emotion management, and relationship nurturing that will be explored in the following books. A woman who has a system for taming her digital world (Book 1) is better equipped to manage the digital distractions that derail her focus (Book 2).

A woman who has reduced her daily stressors through functional organization (Book 1) has more mental and emotional bandwidth to manage the intense feelings and emotional dysregulation that are so prevalent in ADHD (Book 4), and she is less likely to feel overwhelmed by the minor inconveniences that can trigger a disproportionate emotional storm. Similarly, a woman who has a system for managing her responsibilities (Book 1) can reduce the friction in her relationships (Book 5) that so often arises from her neurotypical partner feeling they are taking care of everything on their own.

She can move from a place of reactive chaos to one of intentional, proactive planning, allowing her to build a life that is not just manageable but truly fulfilling.

This book has empowered a woman to recognize that her struggle with organization is not a character flaw, but a neurobiological reality that can be addressed with the right tools and a compassionate, strategic approach. She has learned to break down overwhelming projects into manageable steps, to leverage routines to make maintenance feel less like a chore, and to externalize the cognitive burdens that have left her feeling mentally exhausted for a lifetime. This is a crucial step in her journey toward self-mastery.

A truly organized external life creates a sense of calm and clarity that allows the internal chaos to subside, paving the way for sustained growth, self-acceptance, and genuine well-being.

Reflection questions

- What is the primary emotional cost of disorganization for you (e.g., anxiety, shame, stress)? How can you use "functional organization" as a form of self-care?
- The book discusses the "out of sight, out of mind" phenomenon. What is one area of your physical or digital life where this applies, and what is one visual system you can create to combat it?
- The text suggests breaking down overwhelming tasks into smaller, more manageable steps. Think of one task you've been putting off. What is the single, low-friction first step you can take right now?

BOOK TWO:

SHARPEN YOUR FOCUS:
MASTERING YOUR ADHD BRAIN

INTRODUCTION:

THE PARADOX OF FOCUS

For many women with ADHD, the concept of "focus" is a paradox, a double-edged sword that can feel both like a superpower and a cruel burden. On one hand, a woman's attention can be so scattered that she experiences a "thousand-yard stare," daydreaming or zoning out in conversations or meetings. This can lead to forgetfulness, missed information, and a pervasive sense of being in a fog.

When a topic is intensely stimulating or novel, the ADHD brain can lock into a state of intense, almost obsessive hyperfocus. While this state can lead to incredible bursts of productivity, it is often a source of frustration for partners who feel neglected, as the woman becomes so engrossed in a task that she loses track of time and fails to attend to other responsibilities.

The challenge is not a lack of ability to pay attention, but rather a profound difficulty in regulating it. The issue lies in the brain's struggle to control its "on/off" switch, preventing it from consistently directing its mental spotlight where it needs to be.

The Neurobiological Underpinnings of Attention Dysregulation

The ADHD brain's relationship with attention is distinct and deeply rooted in its neurobiology. This is not a personal failing but a reality of how the brain is wired and how it processes information. Research indicates a significant link between the brain's focus and its dopamine system. Dopamine, a key neurotransmitter involved in motivation, reward, and attention, is often dysregulated in the ADHD brain.

This dysregulation is at the heart of the "on/off" switch of attention. When a task is under-stimulating, the brain struggles to produce enough dopamine to sustain engagement, leading to a desperate search for internal or external novelty.

This is what causes mind-wandering and distractibility. Conversely, a task that provides a constant flow of stimulation, such as a new project or a deeply engaging hobby, can cause a dopamine surge, leading to the state of intense hyperfocus.

The challenge, therefore, is to manage this neurochemical ebb and flow, creating systems that provide the necessary external structure to sustain attention on mundane tasks and prevent hyperfocus from becoming a form of avoidance.

The brain's inability to filter out irrelevant stimuli is a central component of this dysregulation. While a neurotypical brain can effortlessly tune out background noise or visual clutter, the ADHD brain often registers all incoming stimuli with almost equal importance, which is a significant drain on cognitive resources. This struggle with cognitive control, which allows us to regulate attention and ignore distractions, is particularly evident when working memory demands are high.

As a result, the ADHD brain can be easily pulled off course by a phone notification, a colleague walking by, or a fleeting internal thought, making it incredibly difficult to maintain a state of "deep work." This constant battle against a barrage of stimuli creates a significant and measurable cognitive load, which research has shown disproportionately reduces task performance and brain network efficiency in individuals with ADHD compared to their peers without the condition. This constant effort to maintain focus against a brain that is fighting against it leads to a profound sense of "mental fatigue" and being perpetually "frenzied, frazzled, and overwhelmed."

The Dual Edges of Focus: Hyperfocus vs. Inattention

For many women with ADHD, this struggle with focus manifests as two distinct, and often paradoxical, states: a fragmented, scattered inattention and a powerful, almost obsessive hyperfocus. While the world often labels the inattention as a "deficit," it's more accurately a dysregulation of attention, a difficulty in directing and sustaining one's mental spotlight.

Inattention and a Fragmented Mind: The inattentive subtype of ADHD, which is more common in women, is characterized by internalized struggles like daydreaming, a "thousand-yard stare," and a pervasive sense of being in a fog. This can lead to a woman appearing to be disengaged or inattentive in conversations, even when she is genuinely trying to listen, leading her partner or colleagues to feel unheard or unprioritized. This fragmented attention makes it difficult to remember instructions, organize a schedule, or stay on task, all of which are essential for daily functioning. This is not an intellectual deficit, but a difference in how the brain processes and retains transient information, often due to a reduced activation in the prefrontal cortex, which is responsible for remembering task goals and rules.

Hyperfocus: The Superpower with a Catch: Conversely, the ADHD brain can also lock into a state of intense, almost obsessive hyperfocus when a task is intensely stimulating or novel. While this state can lead to incredible bursts of productivity, where a woman might work for hours without noticing the time, it is often a source of frustration for partners and family members who feel neglected.

This is because the hyperfocus is often uncontrolled, leading a woman to become so engrossed in a task that she loses track of time and fails to attend to other responsibilities, such as preparing meals, doing household chores, or engaging in a scheduled activity with her children.

The challenge is that hyperfocus is not a conscious decision to focus, but a reactive state of deep absorption that the brain finds so rewarding it struggles to disengage from it. It's a form of attention dysregulation, not controlled focus, and it can create significant imbalances in a woman's life.

The Cognitive and Emotional Toll of a Fragmented Mind

The daily struggle with attention dysregulation takes a significant toll on a woman's cognitive and emotional well-being. This isn't just about lost productivity; it's about the pervasive feeling of inadequacy, anxiety, and shame that so many women with ADHD report feeling.

Cognitive Load and Mental Fatigue: For a woman with ADHD, the constant effort to filter distractions and sustain focus on mundane tasks is a profound drain on her mental energy. The brain is constantly running on high alert, trying to manage an immense amount of internal and external information without a robust filtering system. This creates a state of chronic mental fatigue, a temporary sluggishness and slowdown of your thinking abilities, which leads to poor focus, carelessness, and forgetfulness. This continuous cognitive effort is often described as the "ADHD tax," a measurable cost that depletes mental energy reserves and makes a woman more susceptible to burnout.

The Emotional Impact on Self-Worth: The persistent difficulties with focus, organization, and follow-through often lead a woman with ADHD to internalize her struggles and blame herself. She may have grown up with a persistent feeling that she is "not an adequate human being" or that there is something personally wrong with her.

She may feel a deep sense of shame when she compares herself to her peers and feels she is not living up to societal expectations of being organized, put-together, and in control. This internalized self-blame, combined with chronic frustrations and a repeated pattern of failures, can contribute to or worsen co-occurring conditions like anxiety and depression.

Focus and the Female Experience: Internalization and Masking

The challenges of attention dysregulation for women are often exacerbated by societal expectations and a greater tendency to internalize their symptoms, rather than externalize them like men. While men are more likely to exhibit the hyperactive and impulsive symptoms that are easier to notice, women often present with the predominantly inattentive subtype, characterized by internalized restlessness and daydreaming that is less obvious to outside observers. This diagnostic disparity is a major reason why women are often underdiagnosed or misdiagnosed in childhood and adulthood.

This internalization of symptoms is directly linked to a practice known as "masking," where women develop sophisticated compensatory behaviors to hide their struggles and appear "neurotypical" to the outside world.

A woman might pretend to take notes in a meeting to hide the fact that she is "zoning out," or she might meticulously maintain a façade of punctuality by building in extra time for everything, a strategy she developed to combat her innate time blindness. This constant, exhausting effort to appear "non-ADHD" is an invisible burden that leads to a lifetime of internalized shame, anxiety, and a shattered sense of self-worth.

Studies confirm that girls are more likely to mask their symptoms than boys, and this can lead to significant negative consequences on their mental health, social functioning, and academic achievement. Masking is a coping mechanism that prevents a woman from feeling seen and understood, often leading to chronic loneliness and a sense of never "fitting in."

The path forward, therefore, is not to force yourself to conform to neurotypical norms, but to build strategies and systems that support your unique brain. It is about moving from a state of reactive distraction to one of proactive, intentional attention. The goal is to stop fighting your brain and to start working with it. This involves recognizing the unique triggers that derail your focus, designing your environment to support deep work, and building an internal toolkit that helps you to anchor your attention in the present moment, even amidst the chaos of a racing mind.

This is how you reclaim control over your mental spotlight and transform your relationship with focus from a source of frustration to a powerful, cultivated skill.

CHAPTER 1:

THE SCIENCE OF FOCUS

The ADHD attentional system is distinct and operates in a way that is profoundly influenced by neurobiology. This is not a personal failing but a reality of how the brain is wired. Research indicates a significant link between the brain's focus and its dopamine system. Dopamine, a key neurotransmitter involved in motivation and reward, is often dysregulated in the ADHD brain.

This dysregulation is at the root of the "on/off" switch of attention. When a task is under-stimulating, the brain struggles to produce enough dopamine to sustain engagement, leading to a desperate search for internal or external novelty. This is what causes mind-wandering and distractibility.

On the other hand, a task that provides a constant flow of stimulation, such as a favorite hobby or a new project, can cause a dopamine surge, leading to the state of intense hyperfocus.

The challenge, therefore, is to manage this neurochemical ebb and flow, creating systems that provide the necessary external structure to sustain attention on mundane tasks and prevent hyperfocus from becoming a form of avoidance.

The Neurobiology of the Attentional System

To truly master focus, it is essential to understand the intricate neurobiological systems at play. The ADHD brain's relationship with attention is distinct and deeply rooted in its neurochemistry. This is not a matter of willpower, but rather a direct result of how the brain processes and prioritizes information.

At the center of this mechanism is dopamine. Often called the brain's "reward" or "motivation" chemical, dopamine is a key neurotransmitter that plays a crucial role in regulating attention and motivation.

Research indicates that individuals with ADHD often have low dopamine levels or a dysregulation in how dopamine is processed, a phenomenon known as the "low dopamine hypothesis". This reduced dopamine signaling can make it exceptionally difficult for the brain to sustain engagement on tasks that are not inherently stimulating or rewarding.

When a task is boring, repetitive, or requires sustained effort, the ADHD brain struggles to produce enough dopamine to find it interesting, leading to a desperate search for internal or external novelty to get that much-needed hit of stimulation.

This is the neurochemical basis for mind-wandering, distractibility, and the constant pull of the "shiny object" syndrome.

This dysregulation also explains the paradox of hyperfocus. When a task is intensely stimulating, novel, or provides immediate and satisfying feedback, it can cause a surge of dopamine. This release of dopamine is so rewarding that the brain locks into a state of intense, almost obsessive hyperfocus, making it difficult to disengage.

While this state can be highly productive, it is often uncontrolled and can lead to the neglect of other responsibilities, as the brain struggles to activate the "off" switch of its mental spotlight. This is why women with ADHD might become so engrossed in a task that they lose track of time and fail to attend to critical duties, leading to frustration for partners who feel neglected. The challenge, therefore, is to manage this neurochemical ebb and flow, creating systems that provide the necessary external structure to sustain attention on mundane tasks and prevent hyperfocus from becoming a form of avoidance.

The neurobiology of ADHD focus also involves other key neurotransmitters and brain networks. Norepinephrine, a close cousin of dopamine, is vital for alertness and arousal, and its dysregulation can impact the brain's ability to maintain an optimal state of readiness for focused work.

Furthermore, the brain's filtering mechanism is often impaired, making it struggle to differentiate between relevant and irrelevant stimuli. This means a phone notification, a fleeting internal thought, or a colleague walking by can all compete for attention with the same intensity as the main task at hand, creating significant cognitive noise and fragmentation.

The Brain's Competing Networks: DMN vs. TPN

Beyond individual neurotransmitters, the ADHD focus challenge can also be understood through the lens of specific brain networks that are responsible for attention and rest. Research has identified two primary networks that play a critical role in our ability to focus: the Default Mode Network (DMN) and the Task Positive Network (TPN).

- **The Default Mode Network (DMN)** is a network of brain regions that is active when the mind is at rest, engaged in daydreaming, mind-wandering, introspection, or thinking about the past and future. It's essentially the brain's "idle" state.

- **The Task Positive Network (TPN)** is the network that becomes active when we engage in focused, goal-directed tasks that require conscious attention and effort.

In a neurotypical brain, these two networks have a reciprocal relationship: when one is active, it suppresses the activity of the other.

When you're focusing on a task, your TPN is on, and your DMN is off. This reciprocal balance allows for the efficient allocation of cognitive resources and helps maintain focus on the task at hand.

However, in the ADHD brain, this balance is often disrupted. The DMN can remain active even when the TPN is supposed to be engaged, leading to a constant internal turmoil of intrusive thoughts, mind-wandering, and a struggle to stay on task. This constant internal "chatter" and the inability to effectively suppress the DMN is a significant source of distraction and cognitive drain for a woman with ADHD.

Another network, the Salience Network (SN), acts as a kind of "switch" between the DMN and TPN, analyzing internal and external information to determine what is most important and requires attention. In the ADHD brain, the connections between these networks can be weaker, which can make it more difficult for the brain to effectively switch from one mode to another.

This explains why it can be hard to initiate a new task (switching from DMN to TPN) or to stop focusing on an engaging task (switching from TPN to DMN) and a brief distraction can often lead to a lengthy derailment, as the brain "sticks" to the new stimulus.

The Cognitive Cost of Attention Dysregulation

The daily struggle with attention dysregulation takes a significant toll on a woman's cognitive and emotional well-being. This is not just about lost productivity; it's about the pervasive feeling of inadequacy, anxiety, and shame that so many women with ADHD report feeling. The constant effort to filter distractions and sustain focus on mundane tasks is a profound drain on mental energy, a phenomenon known as "high cognitive load".

Research confirms that as cognitive load increases, individuals with ADHD experience reduced performance, greater reaction time variability, and reduced brain network efficiency compared to those without the condition.

The brain, already working harder to filter out irrelevant stimuli, becomes overloaded by the sheer volume of visual and sensory information, a significant drain on executive function. This constant battle against a barrage of stimuli creates a profound sense of "mental fatigue" and being perpetually "frenzied, frazzled, and overwhelmed".

This continuous cognitive effort is the "ADHD tax" that depletes mental energy reserves and makes a woman more susceptible to burnout, a phenomenon that research shows is significantly higher in employees with ADHD due to executive function difficulties.

The persistent difficulties with focus, organization, and follow-through often lead a woman with ADHD to internalize her struggles and blame herself. She may have grown up with a persistent feeling that she is "not an adequate human being" or that something is personally wrong with her.

She may feel a deep sense of shame when she compares herself to her peers and feels she is not living up to societal expectations of being organized, put-together, and in control. This internalized self-blame, combined with chronic frustrations and a repeated pattern of failures, can contribute to or worsen co-occurring conditions like anxiety and depression.

The Genetic and Neurobiological Basis

The differences in brain function and chemistry that contribute to ADHD are not a matter of choice, but are rooted in genetics and neurobiology. Research has focused on specific genes that are involved in the regulation of dopamine and other neurotransmitters.

- **Dopamine Transporter Gene (DAT1):** This gene codes for the dopamine transporter protein, which is responsible for the reuptake of dopamine from the synaptic cleft back into the presynaptic neuron. Variations in this gene have been shown to influence the effectiveness of dopamine reuptake, directly impacting the availability of dopamine in the brain and contributing to symptoms of inattention and impulsivity.

- **Dopamine Receptor D4 (DRD4):** This gene is involved in the function of dopamine receptors. Some studies suggest that certain variations of this gene may be associated with learning and working memory disabilities in children with ADHD.

Furthermore, brain imaging studies have found that individuals with impaired focus and memory tend to have reduced activation in specific brain regions, including the prefrontal cortex and cerebellum. The prefrontal cortex, often called the brain's "command center," is responsible for higher-level cognitive functions like attention, working memory, and impulse control. This reduced activity makes it more challenging to remember task goals, instructions, or rules, and contributes to the experience of "brain fog," a temporary sluggishness of thinking abilities that leads to mental exhaustion and poor focus.

This growing body of evidence makes it clear that the ADHD focus challenge is a genuine, neurobiological reality. Understanding this science is the first step toward self-compassion and building effective strategies. It shifts the perspective from a moral failing to a recognition of a genuine neurological difference, paving the way for a more intentional and supportive approach to managing attention.

CHAPTER 2:

DESIGNING YOUR ENVIRONMENT FOR DEEPER CONCENTRATION

Just as a physical environment can be a source of disorganization, it can also be a significant cause of distraction and attention fragmentation for a woman with ADHD. The ADHD brain struggles with filtering out irrelevant stimuli, making it highly susceptible to sensory and visual overload.

The constant hum of a noisy office, a cluttered desk, or a busy view can all pull the mental spotlight off course. To combat this, creating a supportive environment is essential. This involves minimizing visual noise by decluttering and arranging a workspace to face a wall or a serene view. Using tools like noise-cancelling headphones can create a crucial "sound bubble" that helps block out distracting external noise and provides a cue for deep work.

Also, leveraging external accountability can be a powerful tool to initiate and sustain focus. The strategy of "body doubling," where one works alongside another person (either in person or virtually) on their own tasks, has been found to be a highly effective way to combat "activation energy" deficiency. The mere presence of another person provides a subtle sense of accountability and structure, making it easier to start and remain on task without having to rely on willpower alone.

These proactive environmental and social designs reduce the constant mental effort required to fight against distractions, allowing a woman to save her executive function for the actual work.

The Science of Sensory Overload: Why Your Brain Can't Tune Out

For a neurotypical individual, a noisy or cluttered space might be a minor inconvenience, but for a woman with ADHD, it can be a significant source of cognitive and emotional distress. The ADHD brain's neurobiology makes it exquisitely sensitive to sensory input, as it often struggles to filter out irrelevant stimuli with the same efficiency as a neurotypical brain.

This reduced filtering capacity means that a constant barrage of sensory information, be it a flickering light, the hum of an appliance, or a distracting visual, is registered with nearly equal importance as the task at hand. This constant battle against a flood of stimuli creates a significant cognitive load, which research has shown can have a disproportionately negative impact on performance, increase reaction time variability, and reduce brain network efficiency in individuals with ADHD.

This is why a cluttered space or a noisy environment isn't just an inconvenience; it's a direct contributor to reduced cognitive function and task performance.

This struggle with sensory processing can manifest in several key ways, impacting both your ability to focus and your overall emotional state:

- **Auditory Hypersensitivity:** Many individuals with ADHD experience auditory hypersensitivity, clinically known as hyperacusis or misophonia, where routine environmental sounds are not just distracting but can be genuinely distressing or painful. Sounds like a ticking clock, people chewing, or a colleague's tapping keyboard can feel almost unbearable, making it nearly impossible to tune them out and focus on a task. This heightened sensitivity can lead to distress, anxiety, and a constant feeling of being on edge. Using tools like noise-cancelling headphones is a highly effective and evidence-based strategy to create a "sound bubble" that blocks out these triggering noises, allowing your brain to enter a state of deep work without the constant assault of auditory stimuli.

- **Visual Distractions:** Cluttered environments, a messy desk, or a busy view from a window are all powerful visual distractors for the ADHD brain. Each item in your line of sight is a potential mental "ping," demanding a fraction of your attention and consuming valuable working memory resources. This visual noise can increase stress hormones like cortisol, which can in turn exacerbate ADHD symptoms. To combat this, it is essential to minimize visual clutter by clearing your desk of everything not directly related to your current task. Positioning your workspace to face a blank wall can also be an effective strategy to reduce the visual inputs that can pull your mental spotlight off course.

- **The Impact of Temperature and Lighting:** Environmental factors like temperature and lighting can also have a profound impact on focus and cognitive performance for a woman with ADHD. Studies show that being too hot or too cold can significantly impair a person's ability to think and learn, with cognitive ability performing optimally in a temperature range of 20°C to 22°C (68°F to 72°F). Heat exposure, in particular, can worsen ADHD symptoms, increasing irritability, anxiety, and reducing focus by disrupting the brain's delicate balance of neurotransmitters. Similarly, lighting plays a significant role. Natural light is ideal for maintaining focus and promoting a sense of calm, while harsh, flickering fluorescent lights can be overstimulating and contribute to fatigue. Creating a workspace with soft, adjustable lighting can reduce visual strain and create a more soothing atmosphere that supports sustained attention.

Creating Your "Attention Zone": Practical Design Strategies

Your workspace is not just where you do your work; it's a powerful psychological cue for your brain. By intentionally designing a specific "attention zone," you create a clear signal that it's time to focus, reducing the mental friction of constantly having to decide when and where to engage in deep work.

- **Declutter Ruthlessly:** A cluttered physical environment leads to a cluttered mind. The presence of multiple items on a desk, each demanding a fraction of your attention, increases cognitive load and makes it harder to focus. To counteract this, commit to clearing your desk or workspace of everything not directly related to your current task. Implement a "one-touch" rule: if you pick up an item, either take immediate action on it, file it away, or give it a designated "home". This practice frees up cognitive bandwidth by reducing the constant visual scanning and mental processing required to filter out irrelevant items.

- **The Power of a Designated "Home":** A foundational principle of intuitive physical systems is to give every single item a designated "home". This is not about being rigid or a perfectionist; it is a strategic approach to reduce decision fatigue, which is a major drain on executive function. Each time you pick up an item, your brain is faced with a micro-decision: "Where does this go?" By assigning a specific and predictable place for every item, you eliminate this decision-making process. For frequently lost items, such as keys, wallets, and phones, the use of a "landing strip" near the front door is a highly effective strategy that ensures these crucial items are always in a predictable and easily accessible location. This system of predictability reduces the frantic, time-consuming searches that so often accompany ADHD.

- **The "Out of Sight, Out of Mind" Principle:** As mentioned, the ADHD brain can struggle with working memory, a deficit that often leads to the "out of sight, out of mind" phenomenon. This is why traditional organizational advice, such as tucking everything away in opaque boxes, can be completely counterproductive. To counteract this, the organizational system must be intentionally designed to be visual. Using clear storage bins and bold labels allows you to see the contents without having to open them, providing a constant visual cue of what is inside and ensuring your items remain "in mind".

- **Dedicated Work Zones:** If possible, designate a specific area in your home only for deep work. This could be a desk in a corner, a specific chair, or even just a table used only for work during certain hours. The principle here is strong environmental association: your brain learns to associate a certain place with a certain activity. By dedicating a "work zone," you train your brain to enter a focused state merely by being in that area, creating a consistent and reliable cue for focus.

Leveraging External Accountability: The Power of "Body Doubling"

While a well-designed physical environment is critical, some tasks, especially those that are boring, tedious, or require a high degree of sustained effort, can still be incredibly difficult to initiate and complete. For these moments, a powerful strategy for the ADHD brain is to leverage external accountability.

The concept of "body doubling" is a productivity strategy where one works alongside another person on their own tasks. The body double's role is not to help with the work itself, but to serve as a supportive presence that helps the individual with ADHD stay focused and reduce distractions. This strategy is highly effective because it acts as a form of "external executive functioning," providing a stable, non-judgmental anchor for your attention.

Here's a deeper look into why it works and how to implement it:

- **It Provides a Sense of Accountability:** The mere presence of another person, even if they are silent and working on their own task, creates a subtle sense of accountability and pressure. The perception of being "watched" can be a powerful external motivator, making you more likely to follow through on your intended actions without having to rely on willpower alone. The feeling of "I can't waste this gift of time" can be enough to get you started and keep you going.

- **It Models Focused Behavior:** Watching someone else stay focused on a task can naturally encourage the person with ADHD to do the same. The body double becomes a quiet model of control, confidently reflecting the message: "I can concentrate. I am working. I am focused." This modeled behavior is a potent psychological cue that helps you enter a similar state of mind.

- **It Reduces Procrastination and Increases Motivation:** By scheduling a body doubling session, you're proactively setting aside time to work alongside someone else, which makes you more likely to get started when the time comes. This can combat the "activation energy" deficiency that makes task initiation so difficult for the ADHD brain. The novelty of having someone else in the workspace, even virtually, can also add a sense of freshness to a boring routine, which can be helpful since the ADHD brain craves novelty.

- **Virtual Body Doubling:** Body doubling sessions don't have to be in person. Virtual sessions, where you and a partner work together on a video call with your cameras on, have become a popular and effective way to leverage this strategy. This is especially helpful if you're not ready to meet with someone in person or if your schedules don't align. You can each do your own work but keep the call on for accountability and a shared sense of focus.

- **Beyond Body Doubling:** Sometimes, even being in a public space where others are working quietly, like a library or a coffee shop, can create a focused environment. The quiet, productive energy of others can be motivating and act as a passive form of body doubling, helping to anchor your attention.

These proactive environmental and social designs reduce the constant mental effort required to fight against distractions, allowing a woman to save her executive function for the actual work. By intentionally designing your physical and digital environments, and by strategically leveraging external accountability, you are building a system that supports your brain's natural tendencies rather than fighting against them. This is how you create a sustainable, focused, and ultimately more peaceful life.

CHAPTER 3:

MINDFULNESS AND SELF-COMPASSION FOR ATTENTIONAL CONTROL

While external environmental design is crucial, true mastery of focus also requires cultivating an internal toolkit. This is where mindfulness and self-compassion become powerful allies for the ADHD brain. Mindfulness is the practice of paying attention to the present moment without judgment.

For a brain that is prone to racing thoughts, internal restlessness, and a constant stream of new ideas, mindfulness provides a much-needed anchor. It helps a woman become more aware of her thoughts and emotions without becoming entangled in them, providing a crucial pause before she acts on an impulse or gets lost in a mental spiral.

By consistently practicing mindfulness, a woman can learn to gently guide her attention back to her intended focus each time it wanders, which acts as a form of exercise for her attentional muscle.

This practice is deeply intertwined with emotional regulation and distress tolerance. The ability to observe a racing mind or an intense emotion without judgment is the first step toward managing it effectively.

This is particularly important for women with ADHD who often internalize their struggles and feel a deep sense of shame or a lack of self-worth. By approaching her mind with curiosity and compassion, a woman can begin to let go of the rigid expectation that she "should" be able to focus effortlessly. This compassionate stance reduces the anxiety and self-criticism that often accompanies inattentive symptoms, making it easier to re-engage with a task, even after a period of distraction.

The Neurobiological Basis of Mindfulness and the ADHD Brain

Mindfulness for the ADHD brain is not about achieving a perfectly empty, still mind. The ADHD brain is an often overactive, engine of thought, and trying to force it into absolute stillness is often a recipe for frustration and self-criticism. Instead, mindfulness is a form of cognitive training, a practice that builds the brain's capacity for sustained attention and self-regulation over time.

Neuroscientific research supports the efficacy of mindfulness for ADHD by highlighting its ability to influence key brain functions. The ADHD brain is often characterized by a dysregulation in its two primary attentional networks: the Default Mode Network (DMN), which is active during mind-wandering and daydreaming, and the Task Positive Network (TPN), which is active during focused, goal-directed tasks.

In a neurotypical brain, these two networks have a reciprocal relationship, meaning one quiets down when the other is active. However, in the ADHD brain, this balance is disrupted, and the DMN can remain overly active even when the TPN is supposed to be engaged, leading to a constant internal turmoil of intrusive thoughts and mind-wandering.

Mindfulness practice, particularly focused meditation, helps to strengthen the brain's ability to regulate these networks. By repeatedly bringing your attention back to an anchor, such as your breath or a physical sensation, each time it wanders, you are strengthening the neural pathways that are responsible for attentional control and the ability to switch between the DMN and TPN.

This consistent, gentle redirection of focus acts as a form of exercise for the prefrontal cortex, the brain's "command center" for executive functions like attention and impulse control, which is often less active in individuals with ADHD. Over time, this training can make it easier to initiate tasks, sustain attention, and recover from a period of distraction. The practice helps a woman become the observer of her thoughts and emotions, rather than being solely subject to their whims, which is the first step towards self-mastery.

Mindfulness and the Regulation of Emotional Dysregulation

For many women with ADHD, the most debilitating aspect of their condition isn't inattention, but emotional dysregulation. This is a core, significant, and often misunderstood aspect of ADHD, characterized by a heightened emotional intensity and a surprising lack of an internal "buffer" to modulate feelings.

Research suggests that this is due to differences in brain function, particularly in the frontal cortex, which is less likely to inhibit big reactions. This can lead to emotions that feel all-or-nothing, where a woman might hold back her feelings to fit in, but a small trigger can unleash an overwhelming emotional response.

This is where mindfulness becomes a profound ally. The ability to simply observe a racing mind or an intense emotion without judgment is the first step toward managing it effectively. Mindfulness creates a crucial pause between stimulus and response, a space where a woman can recognize the emotion and choose a deliberate action rather than reacting impulsively.

This practice is deeply intertwined with Dialectical Behavioral Therapy (DBT), a highly effective therapeutic approach that combines elements of Cognitive Behavioral Therapy (CBT) with mindfulness techniques to help individuals develop coping skills for managing impulsivity and regulating emotions.

The skills taught in DBT for ADHD are particularly well-suited for women, and mindfulness is the foundational skill upon which the others are built. It helps a woman become more aware of her thoughts and emotions, which can decrease distress and improve her ability to respond effectively to difficult situations. The ability to observe a racing mind or a surge of intense emotion without getting entangled in it is the first step toward gaining a sense of control over it.

Self-Compassion: The Antidote to Shame and the Inner Critic

The journey of living with ADHD for women is often defined by a profound and pervasive sense of shame. This shame is not a symptom of ADHD itself, but a consequence of a lifetime of internalizing struggles and feeling a deep sense of inadequacy. Societal expectations for women to be organized, emotionally mature, and calm create a pressure to conform that directly conflicts with the core symptoms of ADHD.

When a woman with ADHD struggles to maintain order or regulate her emotions, she often internalizes her difficulties and blames herself, a pattern that fuels anxiety, depression, and low self-esteem.

Research suggests that women with undiagnosed ADHD often endure childhoods filled with misunderstanding, self-blame, and a persistent feeling that there is something personally wrong with them, a feeling that is exacerbated by the internal and external pressures they face.

This painful internal dialogue, the "inner critic," becomes a source of stress that can significantly deplete the emotional resources needed for resilience and self-regulation.

Self-compassion is the powerful antidote to this shame. It's the practice of treating yourself with the same kindness, understanding, and support you would offer a good friend in a similar situation. It's acknowledging that your suffering is real and offering comfort, rather than judgment.

For a woman with ADHD, this means letting go of the rigid expectation that she "should" be able to focus effortlessly or get everything done perfectly. It means recognizing that her struggles are a neurobiological reality, not a character flaw.

Practicing self-compassion reduces the anxiety and self-criticism that often accompanies inattentive symptoms, making it easier to re-engage with a task, even after a period of distraction. For example, instead of saying, "I'm so useless for forgetting that," she can rephrase it as, "It's okay to forget things; my brain works differently. What can I do to help myself remember next time?"

This practice of actively cultivating a supportive inner dialogue builds an inner ally who champions her efforts and provides the psychological safety needed to learn from mistakes without being crippled by them. Self-compassion is not self-indulgence; it is the essential fuel that allows for sustainable growth and emotional resilience.

Practical Mindfulness and Self-Compassion Techniques

The power of mindfulness and self-compassion lies in their accessibility. You don't need a dedicated meditation cushion or hours of free time. You can integrate these practices into your daily life in small, manageable ways that work for the ADHD brain.

1. The Breath Anchor: Your breath is always with you and is a constant, subtle sensation. It is perhaps the most fundamental and universally accessible anchor because it is always present, it is neutral, and its rhythm can be both observed and subtly influenced. When you notice your mind wandering, gently bring your attention to the sensation of your breath. Notice the rise and fall of your chest or the feeling of air at your nostrils.

The key is the gentle return of your attention, without judgment, each time it wanders.

Each return is a strengthening of your attentional muscle. A simple practice is to count your breaths, inhaling on "one" and exhaling on "two," up to "ten," and then starting over. This provides just enough mental engagement to keep the ADHD brain from getting bored while still directing attention to the breath.

2. The 5-4-3-2-1 Sensory Grounding Method: This technique is a rapid, powerful circuit-breaker for an overactive mind. When your mind is racing, you feel overwhelmed by internal chatter, or you're stuck in a thought loop, this exercise can quickly ground you in the present by bringing your awareness to external reality.

- **5 things you can see:** Look around and name five distinct things you can see, focusing on details like color, texture, or shape.
- **4 things you can feel:** Notice four things you can feel (e.g., your feet on the floor, the texture of your clothes against your skin, the air temperature, the pressure of your chair).
- **3 things you can hear:** Listen for three distinct sounds (e.g., distant traffic, your own breathing, the hum of a computer).
- **2 things you can smell:** Notice two distinct smells (even if faint).
- **1 thing you can taste:** Notice one taste in your mouth.

This exercise forces your attention outwards, providing a quick reset for your attention and interrupting the emotional spiral.

3. Mindful Movement: For the ADHD brain, which often has physical restlessness, combining mindfulness with movement is an excellent strategy. Instead of seeing fidgeting or restlessness as a sign of failure, you can use it as an anchor for attention.

- **Mindful Walking:** As you walk, shift your attention from your thoughts to the physical sensations of walking. Pay attention to the sensation of your feet touching the ground, the heel-to-toe roll, and the swing of your arms.
- **Mindful Stretching:** Focus intensely on the sensations in your body as you stretch. Notice the stretch, the release, the tension, and the relaxation. This is a great way to combine physical activity with mental anchoring.

4. Compassionate Rephrasing: Actively challenge your inner critic by rephrasing harsh, judgmental thoughts into compassionate and realistic ones.

- **Harsh thought:** "I can't believe I missed that deadline. I'm so useless."
- **Self-compassionate rephrasing:** "It's okay. I missed the deadline. That's a common ADHD challenge. What was the friction point here? What can I learn from this for next time?"
- **Harsh thought:** "I am so lazy; I can't even get started on this chore."
- **Self-compassionate rephrasing:** "This chore feels hard right now. My brain is seeking stimulation. What is one tiny, manageable step I can take right now to get started?"

This is not about ignoring the problem but about approaching it from a place of understanding and solution-oriented thinking rather than self-blame.

Cultivating mindfulness and self-compassion is a lifelong practice, not a quick fix or a destination. It's a journey of continuous learning and gentle redirection. By consistently training your internal toolkit, you'll find it easier to direct your focus where you intend, even in a world clamoring for your attention and a mind prone to wandering.

This internal mastery is a vital complement to designing your external environment, creating a holistic approach that empowers you to truly take command of your attention and, by extension, your emotional well-being and life.

CHAPTER 4:

SINGLE-TASKING AND DEEP WORK STRATEGIES

In a world that praises the illusion of multitasking, a highly effective strategy for the ADHD brain is to embrace single-tasking and cultivate a capacity for "deep work." Multitasking is a myth; what it actually involves is rapid task-switching, a process that is incredibly inefficient and mentally exhausting for the ADHD brain.

The cognitive cost of switching from one task to another is a significant drain on executive function, as the brain must reorient itself and load new information into its working memory each time. To counteract this, a woman can train her brain to focus on one thing at a time.

The Myth of Multitasking and the Science of Task-Switching

For decades, multitasking has been celebrated as a hallmark of efficiency and competence, but neuroscientific and psychological research has decisively debunked this myth. The human brain is simply not built to handle multiple conscious, cognitively demanding tasks simultaneously. Instead, what we perceive as multitasking is actually a process of rapid task-switching, where the brain rapidly shifts its attention between two or more different activities.

For the ADHD brain, which already struggles with attention regulation and executive function, this process of task-switching is inefficient and detrimental. Each time you switch from one task to another, your brain incurs a measurable "task switch cost". This cost involves the mental energy required to disengage from the previous task, reorient your focus, and load new information and rules into your working memory.

This process is incredibly draining and can be a major source of mental fatigue for a woman with ADHD. A 2021 study highlighted that individuals with ADHD experience a reduced amount of cognitive resources available for task-switching, making it far more challenging for them to switch between tasks and complete them efficiently. The frontal lobe, which is responsible for executive functions like working memory and inhibitory control, struggles to disengage from one task and engage with another, leading to a diminished ability to maintain focus and control.

Furthermore, task-switching compromises working memory, sustained focus, and even long-term memory consolidation, and it often leads to a higher rate of errors and a slower working pace. For a woman with ADHD, who may already be prone to careless mistakes and difficulties with memory, this process of constant toggling can become a significant source of frustration, shame, and a sense of being perpetually behind.

Over time, this constant task-switching can overload the brain's attention control system, reducing performance even on single tasks and contributing to a state of chronic mental fatigue. It also puts a significant strain on the prefrontal cortex, which relies on optimal levels of dopamine and norepinephrine to function. When multitasking, the brain may become overstimulated, allowing the amygdala to become more reactive and inhibiting logical reasoning, which further degrades cognitive processing.

The Power of Deep Work: A Counter-Cultural Approach

The antidote to this chaotic, fragmented mode of working is to embrace single-tasking and cultivate a capacity for "deep work." Deep work, a concept coined by author Cal Newport, is the ability to focus without distraction on a cognitively demanding task. It is the kind of work that creates new value, improves your skills, and is difficult to replicate, requiring sustained intellectual effort at the highest level.

For the ADHD brain, deep work is not always easy, but it is profoundly rewarding. The moments of true deep work are where innovation happens, where complex problems are solved, and where significant personal and professional growth occurs. The challenge lies in the ADHD brain's natural inclination towards novelty and immediate stimulation.

A single, demanding task, especially if it involves sustained effort and lacks immediate gratification, can quickly feel boring or difficult, prompting the mind to seek out distractions to get a quick dopamine hit. However, by deliberately engaging in single-tasking and structuring your environment and time for deep work, you can train your brain to embrace sustained effort and achieve higher levels of productivity and satisfaction. You are not fighting your brain but rather teaching it to find reward in sustained, focused effort through structured practice and strategic reinforcement.

This intentional approach to work, which prioritizes impact over "busywork," is a powerful way to move beyond the frustration of a scattered mind and achieve a new level of self-efficacy and accomplishment.

The Pomodoro Technique: Your Anchor for Deep Work

The Pomodoro Technique, developed by Francesco Cirillo in the late 1980s, is one of the most effective and research-backed tools for achieving and sustaining single-task focus for the ADHD brain. It provides a clear, external structure that bypasses the internal difficulties with task initiation and follow-through. The technique involves breaking down a task into short, focused work intervals, traditionally 25 minutes long, followed by a mandatory short break of 5 minutes. After four of these cycles, you take a longer, more restorative break.

The power of this technique for the ADHD brain is multifaceted:

- **It Reduces Overwhelm and Lowers Activation Energy:** The idea of working on a boring or difficult task for an undefined period can be paralyzing, a phenomenon often referred to as "ADHD paralysis." Committing to a task for a short, manageable burst of 25 minutes makes it feel less intimidating and more approachable, making it easier to initiate. This strategic approach reduces the cognitive load of the entire task and provides a clear starting point.

- **It Accommodates the Brain's Need for Breaks:** The scheduled 5-minute breaks provide regular, guilt-free opportunities for the brain to reset and seek novelty without derailing the entire work session. This prevents the mental fatigue and restlessness that can build up during prolonged, static focus. The breaks serve as a reward and a mental reset, accommodating the brain's natural rhythms without allowing them to hijack progress.

- **It Builds Momentum and Provides Rewards:** For the ADHD brain, which is driven by a craving for immediate reward, the Pomodoro Technique provides a satisfying and tangible sense of progress with each completed work interval. This positive reinforcement loop, fueled by small bursts of dopamine from each "win," builds momentum and makes it easier to sustain effort over time. The discipline of single-tasking, enforced by a timer, is a powerful antidote to a scattered mind, allowing a woman to reduce feelings of overwhelm and achieve a higher quality of work with less mental effort. A study found that implementing the Pomodoro technique in a digital marketing company helped employees work more efficiently and improve their work-life balance.

Beyond the Pomodoro: Advanced Strategies for Sustained Focus

While the Pomodoro Technique is a foundational tool, there are other strategies that can be integrated to support consistent follow-through and a capacity for deep work.

- **Batch Similar Tasks:** While the goal is single-tasking within a work session, you can still improve efficiency by batching similar tasks together across your day or week. For example, dedicate a specific block of time solely to answering emails, another block for making phone calls, and yet another for administrative paperwork. This minimizes the "context switching" cost that is so draining for the ADHD brain. By grouping similar activities, you allow your brain to stay in a particular "mode," reducing the friction and cognitive load associated with frequent transitions.

- **The "Pre-Flight Checklist":** Before starting a deep work session, develop a brief, consistent ritual or "pre-flight checklist." This ritual cues your brain that it's time to engage in sustained focus and helps you smoothly transition into deep work. This could include: reviewing your single, specific task for the session, gathering all necessary materials, getting a fresh drink of water, closing all unnecessary programs and tabs, and silencing all notifications. This consistent ritual acts as a psychological trigger, preparing your mind and body for intense concentration and reducing the mental load of having to make these decisions in the moment.

- **Embrace the "Messy Middle":** All projects, especially large ones, have a point where the initial excitement and novelty wear off, and the end isn't yet in sight. This "messy middle" is where many with ADHD abandon projects, as the dopamine hit from novelty fades. Recognize this phase as a normal, predictable part of the creative or productive process. Remind yourself that it's normal to feel less engaged, bored, or frustrated here, and double down on your tiny, actionable steps and leverage your accountability and reward systems to push through this phase.

- **Gamification and Rewards:** The ADHD brain thrives on immediate feedback and rewards. To maintain momentum on a long task, inject elements of a game into your work. Use a timer to "compete" against yourself, create a points system for completed sub-tasks, or build in small, intentional rewards for hitting a milestone. The promise of an immediate, enjoyable reward, like a 5-minute break, a favorite song, or a cup of tea, can provide the necessary dopamine hit to push through a tedious section of a project.

- **Automate and Systemize:** Wherever possible, create systems that reduce the need for conscious effort in follow-through. Set recurring reminders, use templates, or automate routine steps. The less you have to think about it, the more likely you are to do it. The ADHD brain thrives on automation and consistent systems because they reduce decision fatigue and the reliance on inconsistent executive functions. By setting up recurring calendar reminders for tasks that need to be done regularly, for example, you can offload as much routine cognitive load as possible, freeing up your mental energy for deep work.

The commitment to single-tasking and deep work is a powerful counter-cultural act, and it's especially transformative for a woman with ADHD. By deliberately creating mental and environmental space for sustained focus on one thing at a time, you'll not only complete more meaningful work but also experience a profound sense of accomplishment and clarity, moving beyond the chaos of constant distraction.

This intentional approach allows you to harness your considerable potential, achieving a level of productivity and satisfaction that might have previously seemed out of reach.

CHAPTER 5:

SUSTAINING FOCUS AND PREVENTING MENTAL FATIGUE

Sustaining focus is not just about the moment of concentration; it is about intelligently managing one's energy to prevent burnout over the long term. A prominent, but often overlooked, challenge for women with ADHD is a profound sense of "mental fatigue" and being perpetually "frenzied, frazzled, and overwhelmed".

This is not simply a feeling of being tired; it is the result of the constant, conscious effort to manage internalized symptoms, such as a racing mind and emotional dysregulation, that neurotypical individuals do unconsciously. This constant cognitive effort is the "ADHD tax" that depletes mental energy reserves and makes a woman more susceptible to burnout.

For women, this experience is particularly daunting as the demands of work, relationships, and self-care, along with the relentless storm of ADHD symptoms, can pose serious challenges to their mental well-being. Studies show that 58% of employees with ADHD report high burnout levels, a statistic largely attributed to difficulties with executive functions, like attention regulation and emotional control.

Burnout in women with ADHD is a significant cause of stress, frustration, and overwhelm, often caused by trying to mask symptoms and function within systems that are not accommodating to the ADHD brain. This chapter will provide proactive strategies for energy management, ensuring your newfound capacity for concentration is not only powerful but also sustainable.

The Cycle of ADHD Burnout: Understanding the Warning Signs

Burnout is a state of chronic physical, emotional, and mental exhaustion caused by prolonged or excessive stress. It is not just about being tired; it's a deep state of depletion that can leave a woman feeling mentally drained, emotionally numb, and lacking motivation to complete even the simplest of tasks.

For women with ADHD, this can follow a cyclical pattern of intense productivity followed by extreme exhaustion. A woman might hyperfocus on a project for days, neglecting basic needs like food or sleep, which leads to a significant energy debt. This exhaustion then prompts a period of task paralysis and procrastination, which creates an even more urgent need for intense productivity later on, leading to more fatigue and restarting the cycle.

The emotional toll of this cycle is significant. A woman may begin to feel as though her best is not good enough and lose belief in her ability to complete simple tasks. When the cycle sets in, it's common to experience heightened irritability, frustration, mood swings, and an inability to control emotions, sometimes leading to crying spells, yelling, or emotional breakdowns.

Other common signs of burnout include a lack of motivation, emotional detachment, chronic fatigue, headaches, muscle tension, and sleep issues. This cycle is particularly difficult to break because the same ADHD symptoms that contribute to burnout, such as the difficulty with stress regulation, also make it hard to recover. Recognizing these red flags early is the first step toward intervention, allowing you to prioritize rest and self-care before full burnout sets in.

Prioritizing Sleep Hygiene: The Foundation of Focus

For anyone, quality sleep is non-negotiable for cognitive function, but for a woman with ADHD, it is the bedrock of sustained focus, emotional control, and working memory. Research indicates that an estimated 50-75% of adults with ADHD experience sleeping problems, with studies showing that sleep deprivation in ADHD can be as impairing as other adult symptoms combined.

Sleep problems often differ depending on the ADHD subtype: women with predominantly inattentive symptoms are more likely to have a later bedtime, while those with hyperactive-impulsive symptoms are more likely to experience insomnia.

To combat this, a woman must prioritize consistent and healthy sleep hygiene practices.

- **Establish a Consistent Routine:** The human body thrives on regularity, and the ADHD brain is no exception. A consistent bedtime and wake-up time, even on weekends, helps regulate your natural sleep rhythm.
- **Create a Relaxing Ritual:** Your bedtime routine should signal to your body that it's time to wind down. This could include listening to a relaxing audiobook, reading a physical book, taking a warm bath or shower, or practicing deep breathing exercises.
- **Avoid Stimulating Activities:** In the hours before bed, avoid screens, caffeine, sugar, and stimulating work projects that can trigger hyperfocus. The blue light from screens can interfere with melatonin production, while engaging in a highly stimulating task can make it difficult for the ADHD brain to wind down.
- **Clear Your Mental Clutter:** Ruminating on a to-do list or worrying about unfinished tasks can keep you awake. Take time before bed to write out your "to-do" list for the next day, which helps to offload these worries from your mind, allowing

you to relax and fall asleep more easily.

The Proactive Power of Physical Activity

Exercise is not just for physical health; it's a powerful tool for managing ADHD symptoms, regulating mood, and combating mental fatigue. Research has shown that physical activity has a positive effect on inhibitory control in adults with ADHD, and it can also improve cognitive function, emotional state, and mental health. The mechanism behind this is linked to exercise-induced dopamine release, which is associated with improved attention and can help regulate the brain's reward system.

- **Find Your Joyful Movement:** For the ADHD brain, which craves novelty and can struggle with boring, repetitive tasks, finding an activity you genuinely enjoy is key to maintaining a consistent routine. This could be dancing, lifting weights, cycling, hiking, or a team sport.

- **Leverage Both Acute and Chronic Exercise:** Research indicates that both short, intense bursts of exercise (acute) and long-term, consistent physical activity (chronic) have a beneficial effect on inhibitory control. A brisk walk or a short burst of jumping jacks can serve as a powerful "brain break" to combat restlessness and re-energize your focus.

- **Use Exercise to Manage Emotional States:** Physical activity is a direct and healthy way to discharge pent-up emotional energy, which is especially useful for a brain prone to emotional dysregulation. When you feel anger, anxiety, or frustration building, a quick burst of intense movement can act as a physiological "reset button," preventing the emotion from spiraling out of control.

Nourishing Your Brain: Diet and Hydration

What you consume directly impacts your brain's ability to function. Consistent, high-quality fuel is crucial for maintaining stable energy levels, which in turn supports sustained focus and emotional regulation. Dehydration and erratic blood sugar levels can mimic or exacerbate ADHD symptoms, making it even more challenging to stay on track.

- **Mindful Eating:** Focus on balanced meals with lean protein, healthy fats, and complex carbohydrates to maintain steady energy levels. Avoid an excess of sugars and processed foods, which can cause rapid energy spikes followed by a crash that leaves you feeling sluggish and unfocused.

- **The Power of Omega-3s:** Several studies have linked low omega-3 fatty acid levels to common ADHD symptoms like learning difficulties, hyperactivity, and problems with emotional regulation. The brain uses omega-3s as a building block for cell membranes and as a tool to help neurotransmitters carry signals more effectively. Supplementing with omega-3s has been shown to improve mood, reduce hyperactivity, and even enhance working memory.

- **Consistent Hydration:** Being properly hydrated is essential for optimal brain function. Keep a water bottle with you and aim for consistent intake throughout the day rather than large, infrequent amounts. This simple habit can have a significant impact on your focus and mental clarity.

Mindful Breaks and Strategic Pacing

The ADHD brain is not built for sustained, static effort. Pacing yourself and taking mindful breaks is a proactive strategy to prevent overwhelm and cognitive overload before it happens.

- **Build in "Micro-Breaks":** Every 15-20 minutes, take a 30-second to 1-minute brain break. Look away from your screen, stretch, take a few deep breaths, or simply close your eyes. These micro-pauses prevent overstimulation and allow your prefrontal cortex a brief moment of rest.

- **The "ADHD Tax" on Time:** Acknowledge your tendency to underestimate how long tasks will take, a phenomenon known as "time blindness," and add a time buffer of 25-50% to your schedule. This gives you crucial breathing room, reducing the stress that comes from constant rushing and providing a more realistic view of your day.

- **Set Boundaries and Avoid Overcommitment:** Overcommitting is a fast track to overwhelm and burnout for the ADHD brain, as it stretches your executive function resources too thin. Learn to identify your capacity and politely decline requests that will overwhelm you. By protecting your time and energy, you create a buffer against the constant demands of a busy life.

By recognizing that sustained focus is a product of overall well-being, a woman can learn to protect her energy and maintain her newfound capacity for concentration without succumbing to burnout. Proactive self-care is not a luxury but a fundamental necessity for sustainable productivity and emotional well-being. This integrated approach ensures that your sharpened focus becomes a consistent, reliable asset, helping you thrive in a world that constantly vies for your attention, rather than merely survive it.

Conclusion: Your Empowered Attention

This guide has provided a comprehensive framework for sharpening focus, moving from a paradoxical and frustrating experience to a cultivated skill. By understanding the neurobiological underpinnings of inattention and hyperfocus, a woman can stop blaming herself and begin to work with her brain, not against it.

She has learned to design her environment to support deep work, to use mindfulness to anchor her attention internally, and to embrace single-tasking as a more efficient way to work. She also recognizes that true, sustained focus is a product of careful energy management and self-care.

The mastery of these skills empowers a woman to direct her mental spotlight where she wants it to go, rather than being pulled by every fleeting impulse or demand. This provides a profound sense of self-efficacy and a foundation for achieving her goals with greater clarity and control.

From Internal Chaos to Intentional Action: The Foundational Shift

The journey through this book has been a process of profound re-education and self-discovery. For so long, the struggle with attention for a woman with ADHD may have felt like an internal battle, a chaotic torrent of racing thoughts and unyielding distractions. The prevailing narrative, often shaped by societal expectations and a historical lack of research on female ADHD, taught her that her difficulties with focus were a personal failing, a sign of laziness or inadequacy.

This belief system is often at the root of a woman's tendency to internalize her struggles, which, as studies show, can lead to lower self-esteem, self-blame, and a shattered sense of self-worth that is significantly more prevalent in women with ADHD than in their male counterparts.

This book has provided a crucial, liberating shift in perspective by illuminating the neurobiological realities behind these struggles. You have learned that your brain's attentional system is not "broken" but is simply wired differently, a reality deeply rooted in the dysregulation of neurotransmitters like dopamine and the unique interplay of your brain's attentional networks.

You have come to understand that the two sides of your focus, the scattered mind and the state of intense hyperfocus, are not a paradox, but two manifestations of the same core challenge: a difficulty in regulating the brain's "on/off" switch for attention.

This understanding is the bedrock of compassionate self-management. It allows a woman to move past a lifetime of self-recrimination and begin to approach her focus challenges with curiosity and a strategic, problem-solving mindset, rather than with shame and frustration.

The Toolkit of an Empowered Attentional System

This book has not just offered a new perspective; it has provided a concrete, actionable toolkit for transforming this understanding into a cultivated skill. You are now equipped with strategies that work *with* your brain's unique wiring, not against it. The core of this mastery lies in a three-pronged approach: designing your external world to support focus, cultivating an internal toolkit for self-regulation, and building a sustainable foundation of energy management.

1. The Sanctuary of an Optimized Environment: You've learned that your physical and digital environments are not just passive backdrops but active participants in your ability to concentrate. For the ADHD brain, which struggles with filtering out irrelevant stimuli, a cluttered desk, a noisy office, or a constantly pinging phone is not a minor inconvenience—it is a significant source of cognitive overload that reduces performance and efficiency. By learning to design an "attention zone," you have created an external sanctuary that signals to your brain that it is time for deep work. This includes:

- **Minimizing Visual Noise:** Clearing your desk of clutter, facing a blank wall, and using clear storage to combat the "out of sight, out of mind" phenomenon reduces the number of competing stimuli for your mental spotlight.

- **Controlling Sensory Input:** Using tools like noise-cancelling headphones to create a crucial "sound bubble" for the brain that is exquisitely sensitive to auditory input.

- **Leveraging External Accountability:** The simple but powerful strategy of "body doubling," where you work alongside someone else, acts as an external executive function, providing a sense of accountability and a model of focused behavior that helps you initiate and sustain tasks.

2. The Anchor of an Internal Toolkit: The greatest distractions for the ADHD brain often come from within: a racing mind, a flood of new ideas, or an intense emotional surge. This book has provided a framework for cultivating an internal anchor through mindfulness and self-compassion.

- **Mindfulness for Attentional Control:** You have learned that mindfulness is a form of cognitive training that strengthens your ability to gently guide your attention back to your intended focus, acting as a form of exercise for your attentional muscle. This practice helps to regulate the overactive Default Mode Network (DMN), which is responsible for mind-wandering, allowing the brain to more effectively engage its Task Positive Network (TPN) for focused work.

- **Mindfulness for Emotional Regulation:** This practice is deeply intertwined with emotional regulation and distress tolerance, two core challenges for women with ADHD. The ability to observe a racing mind or an intense emotion without judgment creates a crucial pause between stimulus and response, allowing you to choose a deliberate action rather than reacting impulsively. This is a foundational step toward managing the intense emotions that so many women with ADHD report feeling.

- **Self-Compassion as an Antidote to Shame:** For a woman who has internalized her struggles and feels a deep sense of shame, self-compassion is the powerful antidote. By learning to approach her mind with curiosity and kindness, she can begin to let go of the rigid expectation that she "should" be able to focus effortlessly. This compassionate stance reduces the anxiety and self-criticism that so often accompanies inattentive symptoms, making it easier to re-engage with a task after a period of distraction.

3. The Structure for Sustainable Effort: You've learned to abandon the myth of multitasking, recognizing it as a detrimental form of rapid task-switching that is incredibly inefficient and mentally exhausting for the ADHD brain. The discipline of single-tasking is a powerful antidote to a scattered mind, allowing you to achieve a higher quality of work with less mental effort.

- **Deep Work and Single-Tasking:** You have learned to embrace single-tasking and to proactively carve out "deep work" blocks for your most demanding tasks, using a timer to create external structure that reduces overwhelm and makes initiation easier. The Pomodoro Technique provides a clear, manageable structure that makes it easier to initiate and sustain a single task, and its short, scheduled breaks serve as a reward and a mental reset, accommodating the brain's need for novelty without allowing it to derail progress.

- **Energy Management and Preventing Burnout:** You have recognized that true, sustained focus is a product of overall well-being, not just a burst of willpower. A prominent, but often overlooked, challenge for women with ADHD is a profound sense of "mental fatigue" and being perpetually "frenzied, frazzled, and overwhelmed." This constant cognitive effort is the "ADHD tax" that depletes mental energy reserves and makes a woman more susceptible to burnout, a state of chronic exhaustion that research shows is significantly higher in employees with ADHD. To combat this, you have learned to prioritize good sleep hygiene, as quality sleep is critical for attention, emotional control, and working memory. You also recognize that regular exercise serves as a powerful antidote to mental fatigue, as it helps regulate dopamine levels, reduce restlessness, and improve mood.

The Future of Your Focused Edge

The mastery of these skills empowers a woman to direct her mental spotlight where she wants it to go, rather than being pulled by every fleeting impulse or demand. This provides a profound sense of self-efficacy and a foundation for achieving her goals with greater clarity and control.

She is no longer merely coping with her ADHD symptoms but is actively crafting a life that is aligned with her unique strengths and values. This newfound capacity for sustained, intentional focus is a powerful catalyst for growth and achievement, providing a stable and predictable base for the more complex skills of emotion management and relationship nurturing that will be explored in the following books.

- **A Bridge to Emotional Regulation:** The ability to direct your attention is a foundational skill for emotional regulation. The next book, "Master Emotions," will explore how the skills of mindfulness and self-awareness you have cultivated here can be leveraged to create a crucial pause between feeling an intense emotion and reacting to it. You will learn to use your attentional skills to identify and challenge the distorted thoughts that often fuel emotional dysregulation, transforming your relationship with your feelings.

- **A Catalyst for Connection:** The inability to sustain focus in conversations is a common challenge for women with ADHD that can strain relationships. By cultivating a more stable and reliable attentional system, you are better equipped to engage in active, mindful listening, which is the bedrock of meaningful connection. The final book will explore how this sharpened focus can enhance your communication and nurture the deeper bonds that are central to a fulfilling life.

The journey of mastering focus is a continuous practice, not a one-time event. There will be days when the strategies feel effortless and days when the internal chaos feels overwhelming. The true strength lies not in achieving perfection, but in your ability to consistently return to your toolkit, re-engage with your strategies, and approach each challenge with self-compassion. You now have the blueprint to navigate a distracting world with a sharper, more sustained focus, giving you a distinct advantage in all your endeavors. This is the moment you reclaim control over your mental spotlight, and with it, your journey toward a more empowered and intentional life truly begins.

Reflection questions

- This part explores how the ADHD brain's attentional system is not "broken" but is "wired differently". How has this reframing helped you move past self-blame and approach your focus challenges with self-compassion?

- The book discusses the two sides of focus for the ADHD brain: the scattered mind and intense hyperfocus. How can you leverage your capacity for hyperfocus as a strength in your work or hobbies, while also creating systems to manage its challenges?

- The text suggests that proactive self-care is not a luxury but a necessity for sustainable focus. What is one self-care practice you can prioritize this week to protect your mental energy?

BOOK THREE:

BALANCE YOUR HORMONES:
A GUIDE FOR WOMEN WITH ADHD

INTRODUCTION:

THE HORMONAL CONNECTION

For many women with ADHD, living with the condition is not a linear experience; rather, it is a journey profoundly influenced by the natural ebbs and flows of their hormonal cycles throughout their lives.

While this link has been a significant lived experience for countless women for decades, it remains an under-researched topic in the medical community. This lack of understanding can be deeply frustrating, leading to a feeling of not being "believed" when a woman reports that her symptoms worsen during certain times of the month.

This book will address this critical gap, providing an evidence-based discussion that validates a woman's anecdotal experience with scientific research, empowering her to understand and manage this often-ignored aspect of her ADHD. The goal is to move beyond the traditional, male-normed view of ADHD treatment and provide a holistic perspective that accounts for the powerful and dynamic role of hormones.

The Research Gap: Acknowledging the Lived Experience

For too long, the scientific and medical communities have operated under the assumption that ADHD manifests similarly across genders, a misconception rooted in a history of male-centric research. This has created a significant gap in our understanding of the nuances of female ADHD, particularly concerning the powerful influence of hormones. While women have anecdotally reported for years that their symptoms of inattention, anxiety, and emotional dysregulation are exacerbated by hormonal fluctuations, they have often been met with skepticism from healthcare professionals who claim to have "never heard of anything like that."

This lack of belief is not only invalidating but also has tangible, negative consequences. When a woman's hormonal shifts intensify her inattentive symptoms, such as forgetfulness, disorganization, and poor time management, these struggles are often misdiagnosed as anxiety or a mood disorder, leading to ineffective treatment plans and a delayed, or missed, ADHD diagnosis.

A rigorous retrospective study found that the mean age of ADHD diagnosis for females ranged from 16.3 to 28.6 years, compared to 11.2 to 22.7 years for males, underscoring the reality of this diagnostic disparity.

The journey for many women is a lifetime of undiagnosed struggles, fueled by a profound sense of shame and self-blame, before a diagnosis in adulthood finally provides a framework to understand their experience. A key factor in this delay is that women's symptoms are often internalized, such as a "flight of thoughts" or a pervasive sense of internal restlessness, making them less obvious to external observers than the externalized hyperactivity more common in men.

This book provides a critical intervention by shifting the focus from simply validating the symptoms to exploring the neurobiological mechanisms that cause them. It serves as a necessary bridge between a woman's lived experience and the emerging scientific research that is finally beginning to confirm the profound link between hormones and ADHD.

The Neurochemical Link: Estrogen, Dopamine, and the Brain

To understand the profound impact of hormones on ADHD, one must first grasp the intricate link between key sex hormones and the brain's neurochemical systems, particularly dopamine. Research has shown that estrogen, a primary female sex hormone, plays a crucial role in regulating neurotransmitters like dopamine and serotonin.

For individuals with ADHD, dopamine regulation is thought to be different, with lower levels of dopamine in the brain's synapses contributing to symptoms like poor motivation, inattention, and executive dysfunction. Because estrogen can directly influence dopamine levels, fluctuations in this hormone throughout a woman's life can significantly impact the severity of her ADHD symptoms.

For example, lower levels of estrogen are linked to lower levels of dopamine, which can exacerbate core ADHD challenges. This scientific connection provides a powerful explanation for why ADHD can look so different in women at various life stages and why symptoms may feel more severe at certain times.

The relationship is complex, but the key takeaway is that estrogen, in many ways, can be a supportive ally for the ADHD brain. When estrogen levels are high, they can enhance cognitive function and improve mood, often providing a natural boost to a woman's executive functions. However, when estrogen levels drop, this supportive effect diminishes, which can feel like a sudden, and often bewildering, worsening of her symptoms. This understanding is critical because it moves the discussion from a feeling of being "moody" or "overly emotional" to a clear, neurobiological reality that can be observed, tracked, and managed with intention.

The Hormonal Lifespan: From Puberty to Menopause

ADHD in women is not a static condition; it is a dynamic experience that changes across her lifespan in concert with her hormonal journey.

1. Puberty and the Teenage Years: The onset of puberty is a pivotal time when many girls who have previously managed their subtle ADHD symptoms begin to struggle. As sex hormones begin to surge, particularly progesterone and a form of estrogen called estradiol, the balance of the brain's neurochemistry can be significantly disrupted.

This hormonal shift, particularly high levels of progesterone, can prime the brain's emotional center, the amygdala, for a greater reaction. This can lead to increased irritability, impulsivity, anxiety, and depression, making a girl's ADHD symptoms harder to manage and often leading to misdiagnosis as a mood disorder. It can also make stimulant medication less effective, as the fluctuating hormones interfere with the medication's ability to regulate the dopamine system. During this time, boys, in contrast, experience a surge in testosterone that can lead to more externalized, hyperactive symptoms, which are more easily noticed and lead to an earlier diagnosis, further widening the diagnostic gap between genders.

2. The Menstrual Cycle: The natural hormonal fluctuations of the menstrual cycle can have a direct and powerful impact on a woman's ADHD symptoms. Research suggests that attention and executive function can worsen in the low-estrogen, high-progesterone luteal phase of the cycle, which occurs in the days leading up to menstruation. This hormonal environment can lead to increased inattention, anxiety, and stress, and can even make a woman's ADHD medication feel less effective. This experience is so common that it aligns with what many women with ADHD have anecdotally reported for years: that their attention is better before ovulation and can worsen after. The intersection of ADHD and premenstrual symptoms is also significant. A high percentage of women with ADHD also experience Premenstrual Dysphoric Disorder (PMDD), a more severe form of PMS, and the combination of the two conditions can make emotional regulation even more challenging, leading to more pronounced mood swings, irritability, and anger. For women with ADHD, PMDD can heighten feelings of depression, anxiety, and hopelessness, and can lead to more pronounced mood swings and increased anger and irritability, making it even harder to manage emotions. PMDD is also linked to chronic fatigue and sleep issues, both of which can further exacerbate ADHD-related challenges with motivation and concentration.

3. Perimenopause and Menopause: For women in midlife, the hormonal shifts of perimenopause and menopause can present a major and often unexpected challenge. As estrogen and progesterone levels begin to decline, the underlying ADHD symptoms that a woman may have compensated for throughout her life can become unmanageable. Research suggests that this hormonal decline can "unmask" a previously undiagnosed ADHD condition or significantly worsen the symptoms of a diagnosed one, creating what some experts refer to as an "ADHD squared" effect—the compounding of low estrogen and low dopamine. The symptoms of menopause, such as "brain fog," memory lapses, and difficulty with concentration, often mirror the symptoms of ADHD, making it difficult to differentiate between the two conditions and leading to a confusing and frustrating experience. For women with undiagnosed ADHD, perimenopause may be the tipping point when symptoms become too difficult to ignore, leading to increased frustration and self-doubt. It is critical for a woman to understand that the cognitive changes she experiences at this life stage may be directly related to her underlying neurobiology, as this understanding is a vital step toward seeking effective support.

Implications for a Holistic, Personalized Treatment

The link between hormones and ADHD has profound implications for a woman's treatment plan, particularly regarding medication. Many individuals with ADHD who menstruate anecdotally report that the effectiveness of their stimulant medication changes across their menstrual cycle. This aligns with the hypothesis that fluctuating hormonal status can directly influence the effectiveness of ADHD medication, as hormones like estrogen can impact the dopamine system that these medications target.

This growing body of evidence has led to the development of potential new approaches to treatment, such as "cycle dosing," where medication dosages are tailored to a woman's hormonal status. While research in this area is still in its early stages, it empowers a woman to take control of her treatment by tracking her own symptoms and their relationship to her cycle.

By keeping a detailed log of her symptoms, she can gather concrete data to present to her doctor, validating her experience and advocating for a more personalized, effective treatment plan that addresses her unique neurobiological needs across her lifespan. This holistic approach ensures that her treatment is not a static prescription but a dynamic, lifelong process that accounts for her unique and fluctuating hormonal profile.

Beyond medication, a woman can also implement proactive lifestyle strategies to help manage the cognitive and emotional symptoms that arise from hormonal fluctuations. A holistic approach that supports both the brain and the body is essential for building resilience. Regular physical exercise is a powerful tool, as it helps regulate mood and brain function, reduces stress, and improves sleep quality.

Good sleep hygiene is also a critical component, as sleep is vital for attention, emotional control, and working memory, and a lack of it can exacerbate hormonal imbalances and ADHD symptoms. Nutrition plays a significant role in brain health and mood stability. The consumption of foods rich in omega-3 fatty acids, antioxidants, and protein can help support brain function and stabilize mood and energy levels. A conscious effort to reduce sugars and processed foods can also help to prevent the energy crashes that exacerbate ADHD symptoms.

Finally, managing stress through mindfulness and other techniques is crucial, as high stress levels can further disrupt hormonal balance and cognitive function. By consistently engaging in these self-care strategies, a woman can build a buffer against the hormonal ebbs and flows and create a more stable and supportive internal environment for her ADHD brain.

This book will provide a groundbreaking discussion on the critical, yet understudied, link between hormones and ADHD in women. It has validated the lived experience of countless women who have anecdotally reported that their symptoms are profoundly impacted by their hormonal cycles. By understanding the neurochemical connection, navigating the challenges of the menstrual cycle and menopause, and exploring tailored treatment and self-care strategies, a woman can move from feeling powerless against her symptoms to a place of informed action.

This holistic approach ensures that her treatment plan is not a static prescription but a dynamic, lifelong process that accounts for her unique neurobiological needs. This understanding is a crucial step towards achieving genuine balance and well-being.

CHAPTER 1:

THE NEUROCHEMICAL LINK

To understand the profound impact of hormones on ADHD, one must first grasp the intricate link between key sex hormones and the brain's neurochemical systems, particularly dopamine. Research has shown that estrogen, a primary female sex hormone, plays a crucial role in regulating neurotransmitters like dopamine.

For individuals with ADHD, dopamine regulation is thought to be different, with lower levels of dopamine in the brain's synapses contributing to symptoms like poor motivation, inattention, and executive dysfunction. Because estrogen can directly influence dopamine levels, fluctuations in this hormone throughout a woman's life can significantly impact the severity of her ADHD symptoms.

For example, lower levels of estrogen are linked to lower levels of dopamine, which can exacerbate core ADHD challenges. This scientific connection provides a powerful explanation for why ADHD can look so different in women at various life stages and why symptoms may feel more severe at certain times.

The Role of Dopamine: The Brain's Fuel for Focus and Motivation

At the very core of the ADHD experience lies a distinct neurochemical reality, and dopamine is at its center. Often called the brain's "reward" or "motivation" chemical, dopamine is a key neurotransmitter that plays a crucial role in regulating attention, motivation, and executive functions like planning and focus.

Research indicates that individuals with ADHD often have low dopamine levels or a dysregulation in how dopamine is processed within the brain, a phenomenon known as the "low dopamine hypothesis". This reduced dopamine signaling makes it exceptionally difficult for the brain to sustain engagement on tasks that are not inherently stimulating or rewarding. When a task is boring, repetitive, or requires sustained effort, the ADHD brain struggles to produce enough dopamine to find it interesting, leading to a desperate search for internal or external novelty to get that much-needed hit of stimulation.

This is the neurochemical basis for mind-wandering, distractibility, and the constant pull of the "shiny object" syndrome that so many women with ADHD report feeling.

The brain's ability to focus is also directly tied to the efficiency of its neurotransmitter systems. When these systems are dysregulated, the brain's filtering mechanism can be impaired, making it struggle to differentiate between relevant and irrelevant stimuli. This means that a constant barrage of sensory information, be it a flickering light, the hum of an appliance, or a distracting visual, is registered with nearly equal importance as the task at hand.

This persistent battle against a flood of stimuli creates a significant cognitive load, which research has shown can have a disproportionately negative impact on performance, increase reaction time variability, and reduce brain network efficiency in individuals with ADHD. The constant effort to maintain focus against a brain that is fighting against it leads to a profound sense of "mental fatigue" and being perpetually "frenzied, frazzled, and overwhelmed".

Estrogen and its Influence on the Dopamine System

The female hormonal cycle introduces a powerful, dynamic variable into this neurochemical equation. Estrogen, a primary female sex hormone, plays a crucial role in regulating dopamine and other key neurotransmitters like serotonin and norepinephrine. Research has consistently shown that higher levels of estrogen are linked to increased levels of dopamine, which can have a supportive effect on the brain's attentional and emotional systems. This can feel like a natural cognitive and emotional boost, where a woman's executive functions are slightly more robust, and her mood is more stable.

Conversely, when estrogen levels drop, this supportive effect diminishes, which can feel like a sudden, and often bewildering, worsening of her ADHD symptoms. Lower levels of estrogen are linked to lower levels of dopamine, which can exacerbate core ADHD challenges like poor motivation, inattention, and executive dysfunction. This relationship provides a powerful, scientific explanation for what countless women have anecdotally reported for years: that their ability to focus, their energy levels, and their emotional stability are directly tied to the ebb and flow of their hormonal cycles.

The influence of hormones is so profound that it can even impact the effectiveness of ADHD medication. Many individuals with ADHD who menstruate anecdotally report that the effectiveness of their stimulant medication changes across their menstrual cycle. This aligns with the hypothesis that fluctuating hormonal status can directly influence the effectiveness of ADHD medication, as hormones like estrogen can impact the dopamine system that these medications target.

By understanding this, a woman can begin to track her symptoms and their relationship to her cycle, gathering concrete data to have a more informed conversation with her doctor about potential new approaches, such as "cycle dosing," where medication dosages are tailored to her hormonal status.

The Complicating Factor: The Role of Progesterone

While estrogen is often the star player in this hormonal conversation, progesterone, the other major female sex hormone, also plays a significant and often complicating role. Progesterone levels are typically low during the follicular phase of the menstrual cycle but rise significantly during the luteal phase, which occurs in the days leading up to menstruation.

Research suggests that high levels of progesterone can moderate or even negate some of estrogen's positive emotional and cognitive benefits. This is because high progesterone can prime the amygdala, the brain's emotional center, for a greater reaction, which can lead to increased irritability, impulsivity, anxiety, and depression.

The combination of low estrogen and high progesterone that occurs during the luteal phase can create a particularly challenging environment for the ADHD brain, exacerbating symptoms and making a woman more susceptible to emotional dysregulation, anxiety, and stress.

This complex hormonal interplay provides a clear neurobiological basis for why many women feel that their symptoms worsen in the days leading up to their period. The intersection of ADHD and Premenstrual Dysphoric Disorder (PMDD) is also significant, with a high percentage of women with ADHD also experiencing PMDD, a more severe form of PMS that is characterized by intense emotional symptoms like depression, anxiety, and anger.

The combination of these two conditions can make emotional regulation even more challenging, leading to more pronounced mood swings, irritability, and anger.

Genetic Influences on Dopamine and Hormonal Sensitivity

The interplay between hormones and neurochemistry is further complicated by genetics. Research has focused on specific genes that are involved in the regulation of dopamine and other neurotransmitters. The Dopamine Transporter Gene (DAT1) and the Dopamine Receptor D4 (DRD4) genes are two of the most well-studied candidates. The DAT1 gene codes for the dopamine transporter protein, which is responsible for the reuptake of dopamine from the synaptic cleft back into the presynaptic neuron. Variations in this gene have been shown to influence the effectiveness of dopamine reuptake, directly impacting the availability of dopamine in the brain and contributing to symptoms of inattention and impulsivity.

Similarly, certain variations of the DRD4 gene, which is involved in the function of dopamine receptors, have been associated with difficulties in working memory and other cognitive functions in children with ADHD.

This intricate genetic basis means that a woman's sensitivity to hormonal fluctuations may not be uniform. Some women may be more genetically predisposed to experiencing significant symptom exacerbation during periods of low estrogen due to a particular genetic variation, while others may be less affected. This is a complex interplay of genetics, hormones, and environmental factors that creates a unique neurobiological profile for each woman.

The "ADHD Squared" Effect: Perimenopause and Menopause

The hormonal influence on ADHD culminates in midlife, during the transition into perimenopause and menopause, presenting a major and often unexpected challenge. As estrogen and progesterone levels begin to decline, the underlying ADHD symptoms that a woman may have compensated for throughout her life can become unmanageable.

Research suggests that this hormonal decline can "unmask" a previously undiagnosed ADHD condition or significantly worsen the symptoms of a diagnosed one, creating what some experts refer to as an "ADHD squared" effect, the compounding of low estrogen and low dopamine.

The symptoms of perimenopause, such as "brain fog," memory lapses, and difficulty with concentration, often mirror the symptoms of ADHD, making it difficult to differentiate between the two conditions and leading to a confusing and frustrating experience.

A woman might wonder if she is developing early-onset dementia or if her struggles are a normal part of aging, when in fact, they may be directly related to her underlying neurobiology. This is why it is critical for a woman to understand this link, as it provides a clear, actionable pathway toward seeking effective support.

This growing body of evidence makes it clear that the ADHD focus challenge is a genuine, neurobiological reality. Understanding this science is the first step toward self-compassion and building effective strategies. It shifts the perspective from a moral failing to a recognition of a genuine neurological difference, paving the way for a more intentional and supportive approach to managing attention.

The Path Forward: From Anecdote to Action

The journey of living with ADHD for women has long been marked by a feeling of not being believed, with their experiences dismissed as a character flaw or a mood disorder. This lack of understanding is a direct result of a research gap that has historically focused on a male-normed view of ADHD. However, the emerging research on the neurochemical link between hormones and ADHD provides a powerful framework for change.

It validates a woman's anecdotal experience with scientific evidence, empowering her to take control of her health and advocate for a more personalized, holistic approach to treatment that accounts for her unique and dynamic neurobiological needs.

This knowledge is not just for healthcare providers; it is a vital tool for every woman with ADHD. By understanding the neurochemical and hormonal interplay, a woman can become an expert on her own body and mind.

She can begin to track her symptoms in relation to her cycle, her sleep, and her stress levels, gathering the data needed to make informed decisions about her well-being. This is how she can move from feeling powerless against her symptoms to a place of informed action and genuine self-mastery.

This chapter has provided the foundational scientific context for this journey, and the following chapters will build on this understanding, offering a practical roadmap for navigating the hormonal fluctuations of the menstrual cycle and menopause, and for exploring tailored, evidence-based strategies for a more balanced and fulfilling life.

CHAPTER 2:

NAVIGATING THE MENSTRUAL CYCLE

The natural hormonal fluctuations of the menstrual cycle can have a direct and powerful impact on a woman's ADHD symptoms. Research suggests that attention and executive function can worsen in the low-estrogen, high-progesterone luteal phase of the cycle, which occurs in the days leading up to menstruation. This hormonal environment can lead to increased inattention, anxiety, and stress, and can even make a woman's ADHD medication feel less effective. This experience is so common that it aligns with what many women with ADHD have anecdotally reported for years: that their attention is better before ovulation and can worsen after.

The intersection of ADHD and premenstrual symptoms is also significant. A high percentage of women with ADHD also experience

Premenstrual Dysphoric Disorder (PMDD), and the combination of the two conditions can make emotional regulation even more challenging, leading to more pronounced mood swings, irritability, and anger. By learning to track her menstrual cycle and its impact on her symptoms, a woman can gain valuable insights to help her proactively manage her energy, plan her schedule, and have a more informed conversation with her doctor.

The Hormonal Landscape of the Menstrual Cycle

To effectively navigate the impact of the menstrual cycle on ADHD symptoms, it is crucial to understand the two main phases and the hormones that dominate them. The two primary hormones at play are estrogen and progesterone, both of which fluctuate in a predictable pattern each month and have a direct line to the brain's emotional and cognitive centers. The brain is filled with receptors for these hormones, and their levels directly influence the brain's neurotransmitter systems, particularly dopamine, which is heavily implicated in ADHD.

The menstrual cycle can be broadly divided into two main phases:

- **The Follicular Phase:** This phase begins on the first day of menstruation and lasts until ovulation, around day 14 of a typical cycle. During this time, estrogen levels gradually rise. For many women with ADHD, this can be a period of relative calm and improved functioning. Because higher levels of estrogen are linked to increased levels of dopamine, this phase can offer a welcome boost of energy, a better mood, and greater cognitive clarity. Women may feel more focused, motivated, and emotionally stable, which can make it a productive and positive time of the month.

- **The Luteal Phase:** This phase begins after ovulation and lasts until menstruation. Progesterone levels are low during the follicular phase but rise significantly in the luteal phase, while estrogen levels drop after ovulation and then decrease again in the days leading up to menstruation. This low-estrogen, high-progesterone environment can be particularly challenging for the ADHD brain. As the supportive effects of estrogen diminish, symptoms of inattention, poor planning, and executive dysfunction can become more pronounced. This is often the time when women feel a noticeable worsening of their ADHD symptoms, making it harder to focus, manage daily tasks, and regulate their emotions. This aligns with what many women anecdotally report: their attention is better before ovulation and can worsen after.

The relationship between these hormones is so powerful that a woman's hormonal status can influence her ADHD symptoms, medication effectiveness, and overall functioning across her entire lifespan, from puberty through to menopause.

The Intersection of ADHD and Premenstrual Dysphoric Disorder (PMDD)

The premenstrual or late luteal phase is not just a time of poor attention and increased anxiety; for a significant number of women with ADHD, it is a period of profound emotional and physical distress. Research indicates that over 40% of women with ADHD also experience Premenstrual Dysphoric Disorder (PMDD), a more severe form of premenstrual syndrome (PMS). This high rate of co-occurrence highlights how closely these two conditions are connected and how powerfully they can overlap.

PMDD is characterized by at least one significant emotional symptom, which can include strong feelings of depression and hopelessness, significant anxiety or tension, and persistent anger or irritability that can cause conflicts in relationships. Both ADHD and PMDD are linked to changes in brain function and hormones, and their combination can create a perfect storm of emotional dysregulation.

For a woman with ADHD who already struggles with emotional intensity and a lack of an internal "buffer" to modulate feelings, the added burden of PMDD can make emotional regulation even more challenging. This can lead to more pronounced mood swings, irritability, and anger, making it difficult to manage emotions and maintain a sense of control.

PMDD also brings a host of other symptoms that directly compound the challenges of ADHD:

- **Exhaustion and Low Energy:** PMDD is linked to sleep disturbances, fatigue, and low energy, which can further lower motivation and make it even harder for a woman with ADHD to get things done.
- **Cognitive Difficulties:** The brain fog and forgetfulness associated with PMDD can become even more pronounced when combined with the working memory and inattention issues of ADHD. This compounds the typical focus-related challenges a woman faces, making it harder to stay focused, organize tasks, and follow through on instructions.
- **Physical Symptoms:** PMDD symptoms can also be physical, including headaches, muscle or joint pain, and bloating, all of which can increase a woman's discomfort and make it more challenging to manage her daily responsibilities.

The combination of these conditions can make the emotional and physical toll of the premenstrual phase feel unbearable. By understanding this link, a woman can stop blaming herself for what feels like a "meltdown" and start developing proactive strategies to manage this difficult period with greater self-compassion and support.

Hormones and Medication Efficacy: A Personalized Approach

The intricate link between hormones and ADHD has profound implications for a woman's treatment plan, particularly regarding medication. Many individuals with ADHD who menstruate anecdotally report that the effectiveness of their stimulant medication changes across their menstrual cycle. This aligns with the hypothesis that fluctuating hormonal status can directly influence the effectiveness of ADHD medication, as hormones like estrogen can impact the dopamine system that these medications target.

Research on this front is limited, but a rigorous study that is pioneering a new stage of work has been designed to directly examine the role of circulating estrogen in relation to ADHD symptoms in young women.

Preliminary data from this study suggests that for women with greater ADHD symptoms, within-person declines in estrogen, particularly in the context of rising progesterone levels just after ovulation, are associated with clinically significant increases in ADHD symptoms. The results of such work have the potential to change clinical practice by indicating the need to account for cycle phase in ADHD evaluations and to suggest personalized approaches to treatment targeted to a woman's unique hormone levels.

This emerging body of evidence has led to the development of potential new approaches, such as "cycle dosing," where medication dosages are tailored to a woman's hormonal status. While this is still an area of active research, it empowers a woman to take control of her treatment by tracking her own symptoms and their relationship to her cycle.

By keeping a detailed log of her symptoms, she can gather concrete data to present to her doctor, validating her experience and advocating for a more personalized, effective treatment plan that addresses her unique neurobiological needs across her lifespan.

Proactive Strategies for Managing Your Cycle

The knowledge of how your hormones impact your ADHD is only truly powerful when it is paired with a proactive plan of action. The goal is not to fight against your cycle but to work with it, creating systems that provide support when you need it most.

- **Track Your Symptoms:** The first step is to become a detective of your own body and mind. Use a simple journal or a dedicated tracking app to record your ADHD symptoms each day. Note your energy levels, focus, motivation, emotional state, and the effectiveness of your medication. Be sure to also track your menstrual cycle, marking the days of your period and when you ovulate. Over two to three months, you will begin to see clear patterns emerge, providing you with invaluable data to anticipate your more challenging days and plan accordingly.

- **Plan Your Schedule with Your Cycle in Mind:** Once you have a clear understanding of your patterns, you can begin to strategically plan your schedule. For instance, if you know that the luteal phase is particularly challenging for you, avoid scheduling major projects, difficult conversations, or demanding social events during that time. Instead, front-load your more cognitively demanding tasks in the follicular phase and save more routine, low-energy tasks for the days leading up to your period. This approach reduces frustration and guilt by working with your natural rhythms.

- **Prioritize Proactive Self-Care:** Your self-care routine should be a non-negotiable part of your monthly cycle, especially during the more challenging phases. Regular physical activity, even just a brisk walk, can serve as a powerful antidote to mental fatigue, help regulate dopamine levels, reduce restlessness, and improve mood. Consistent and high-quality sleep is critical for attention, emotional control, and working memory, and a lack of it can exacerbate hormonal imbalances and ADHD symptoms. Nutrition also plays a significant role. Focusing on a diet rich in omega-3 fatty acids, antioxidants, and protein can help support brain function and stabilize mood and energy levels, while a conscious effort to reduce sugars and processed foods can help prevent the energy crashes that exacerbate ADHD symptoms.

- **Communicate and Set Boundaries:** Openly and gently communicate with your partner, family, and close friends about the impact your cycle has on you. This isn't about making excuses, but about fostering empathy and understanding. You can say, "The week before my period is often difficult for me, so I may be more irritable or forgetful. It's not personal, but I'll need a little more space and support during that time." This proactive communication can reduce conflict and resentment by setting clear expectations.

- **Have a Crisis Plan for Intense Days:** On days when you feel an emotional storm brewing, have a plan of action ready to go. This could include a pre-planned calming activity, like a hot bath or listening to a specific playlist, a list of people you can reach out to, or an "exit strategy" for social situations that feel overwhelming. Having a pre-defined plan reduces the need for difficult decision-making in the moment of crisis.

By consistently applying these proactive, evidence-based strategies, a woman can move from feeling powerless against her symptoms to a place of informed action. This holistic approach ensures that her treatment plan is not a static prescription but a dynamic, lifelong process that accounts for her unique neurobiological needs. This understanding is a crucial step towards achieving genuine balance and well-being.

CHAPTER 3:

THE TRANSITION YEARS: PERIMENOPAUSE, MENOPAUSE, AND COGNITIVE CHANGE

For women in midlife, the hormonal shifts of perimenopause and menopause can present a major and often unexpected challenge. As estrogen and progesterone levels begin to decline, the underlying ADHD symptoms that a woman may have compensated for throughout her life can become unmanageable.

Research suggests that this hormonal decline can "unmask" a previously undiagnosed ADHD condition or significantly worsen the symptoms of a diagnosed one, creating what some experts refer to as an "ADHD squared" effect: the compounding of low estrogen and low dopamine.

The symptoms of menopause, such as "brain fog," memory lapses, and difficulty with concentration, often mirror the symptoms of ADHD, making it difficult to differentiate between the two conditions and leading to a confusing and frustrating experience. This is why it is critical for a woman to understand that the cognitive changes she experiences at this life stage may be directly related to her underlying neurobiology.

Table: The Impact of Hormones on ADHD Symptoms Across the Female Lifespan

Phase of Life	Key Hormonal Changes	Corresponding ADHD Symptom Changes	Neurochemical Link
Childhood	Hormone levels are low and consistent	Symptoms are often more consistent, which can make treatment easier	Stable hormones lead to more predictable brain chemistry.
Puberty	Sharp increase in progesterone and estrogen	Symptoms can become harder to manage, with increased irritability and impulsivity	High progesterone can impact brain regions related to emotion, while testosterone in boys may lead to externalized symptoms.
Menstrual Cycle	Estrogen and progesterone fluctuate monthly	Symptoms may worsen during the low-estrogen luteal phase, leading to more inattention, anxiety, and mood swings.	Lower estrogen is linked to lower dopamine levels, which can exacerbate ADHD symptoms.

Phase of Life	Key Hormonal Changes	Corresponding ADHD Symptom Changes	Neurochemical Link
Perimenopause & Menopause	Gradual decline in estrogen and progesterone	Symptoms may become unmanageable, including worsening inattention, poor time management, and emotional dysregulation. Previously subthreshold symptoms can become highly apparent.	The combination of declining estrogen and low dopamine creates a compounding effect, or "ADHD squared".

CHAPTER 4:

HORMONES, MEDICATION EFFICACY, AND TAILORED TREATMENT

The link between hormones and ADHD has profound implications for a woman's treatment plan, particularly regarding medication. Many individuals with ADHD who menstruate anecdotally report that the effectiveness of their stimulant medication changes across their menstrual cycle. This aligns with the hypothesis that fluctuating hormonal status can directly influence the effectiveness of ADHD medication, as hormones like estrogen can impact the dopamine system that these medications target.

This growing body of evidence has led to the development of potential new approaches to treatment, such as "cycle dosing," where medication dosages are tailored to a woman's hormonal status.

While research in this area is still limited and in its early stages, it empowers a woman to take control of her treatment by tracking her own symptoms and their relationship to her cycle. By keeping a detailed log of her symptoms, she can gather concrete data to present to her doctor, validating her experience and advocating for a more personalized, effective treatment plan that addresses her unique neurobiological needs across her lifespan.

The Neurochemical Basis for Medication Efficacy Fluctuations

For a woman with ADHD, the journey of finding an effective medication and a stable dose is often a long and arduous one. But even after finding a regimen that seems to work, many women anecdotally report that their medication's efficacy fluctuates throughout the month. This isn't an imagined experience; it has a clear neurochemical basis. As discussed, estrogen plays a crucial role in regulating dopamine, the key neurotransmitter targeted by stimulant medications used to treat ADHD.

The effectiveness of stimulant medication is tied to its ability to increase dopamine availability in the brain's synapses, thereby improving attention, motivation, and executive function. When estrogen levels are high, they can enhance dopamine levels, which can have a supportive effect on the brain's attentional systems and may potentiate the effects of medication.

When estrogen levels drop, particularly in the low-estrogen luteal phase that precedes menstruation, this supportive effect diminishes. The drop in estrogen can be linked to lower levels of dopamine, which can exacerbate core ADHD challenges and make the medication feel less effective.

This biological shift can feel like hitting a wall, where a woman's medication suddenly stops working as it should, leading to a frustrating return of her inattentive symptoms, anxiety, and a feeling of being out of control. It's a common experience that a woman's attention is better before ovulation and can worsen after.

This link is so profound that some women with ADHD who have predominantly inattentive symptoms report a significant worsening of their symptoms during the luteal phase. They may experience more pronounced difficulties with planning, organizing, and focusing, while also feeling a greater sense of anxiety and stress. This is further complicated for women with ADHD who also experience Premenstrual Dysphoric Disorder (PMDD), as the combination of the two conditions can make emotional regulation even more challenging, leading to more pronounced mood swings, irritability, and anger.

This is why it is so critical for a woman to recognize that her struggles during this time are not a personal failing but a neurobiological reality that can be managed with a tailored approach.

The Call for Personalized Treatment: The Rise of "Cycle Dosing"

The traditional, male-normed approach to ADHD treatment often involves a static medication dose that is expected to be effective every day of the month. However, a woman's brain chemistry is not static; it is a dynamic landscape that changes with her hormonal cycle. This disconnect between a static treatment plan and a dynamic reality is at the heart of many women's struggles.

A growing body of anecdotal evidence from women, combined with emerging research, is leading to the development of potential new approaches to treatment, such as "cycle dosing." This approach involves tailoring medication dosages to a woman's hormonal status, for example, by slightly increasing her dose during the low-estrogen luteal phase when her symptoms are most pronounced. While research in this area is still limited and in its early stages, it empowers a woman to take control of her treatment by tracking her own symptoms and their relationship to her cycle.

The results of studies pioneering this new work have the potential to change clinical practice by indicating the need to account for a woman's cycle phase in ADHD evaluations, and to suggest personalized approaches to treatment targeted to her unique hormone levels.

The need for personalized treatment extends beyond the menstrual cycle. For women in midlife, the hormonal shifts of perimenopause and menopause can present a major and often unexpected challenge. As estrogen and progesterone levels decline, underlying ADHD symptoms that a woman may have compensated for throughout her life can become unmanageable.

This hormonal decline can "unmask" a previously undiagnosed ADHD condition or significantly worsen the symptoms of a diagnosed one, creating what some experts refer to as an "ADHD squared" effect: the compounding of low estrogen and low dopamine. A woman may feel that her stimulant medication, which once worked well, is now much less effective at a time in her life when she is dealing with significant cognitive changes like "brain fog" and memory lapses. This is why an informed discussion with a doctor about medication and dosage is critical at this life stage.

Empowering Your Voice: Tracking Symptoms to Advocate for Yourself

For years, women who reported a link between their menstrual cycle and ADHD symptoms were often told by doctors that they "had never heard of anything like that." This profound lack of understanding and belief from the medical community can leave a woman feeling invalidated, hopeless, and alone. To move past this, a woman must become an expert on her own body and mind, gathering concrete, objective data to back up her subjective experience.

The most powerful tool for this is a detailed symptom log. By diligently tracking her symptoms, a woman can transform her experience from a collection of vague feelings into a clear, visual, and measurable pattern that can be presented to a doctor.

This process turns a subjective report of "I'm more tired and irritable" into an objective report of "My inattention, anxiety, and fatigue scores were consistently 40% higher during the five days leading up to my period for the last three months, and my medication's effectiveness was reduced by 50% during that time."

By keeping a detailed log of her symptoms, she can:

- **Identify Her Unique Patterns:** She will begin to see clear, consistent patterns in how her symptoms, emotional regulation, energy levels, and medication efficacy are influenced by her cycle. This self-knowledge is the first step toward a proactive, rather than reactive, approach to her well-being.

- **Validate Her Experience:** The data she collects provides undeniable evidence of a correlation between her hormonal status and her ADHD symptoms, which can be crucial for an informed discussion with a healthcare provider who may be unaware of this link.

- **Advocate for a Personalized Plan:** With this data in hand, a woman is in a powerful position to advocate for a more personalized treatment plan, whether that involves a discussion about cycle dosing, a conversation about non-medication strategies to implement during her more challenging days, or a comprehensive review of her overall well-being.

This process of tracking is a vital step toward an empowered and informed approach to treatment. It is about moving from a place of feeling powerless against her symptoms to a place of informed action, ensuring that her treatment plan is not a static prescription but a dynamic, lifelong process that accounts for her unique and fluctuating neurobiological needs. This understanding is a crucial step toward achieving genuine balance and well-being.

A Holistic Approach: The Synergy of Medication and Self-Care

The conversation around medication efficacy and hormones is not just about dosage adjustments; it's about a holistic approach that recognizes the synergy between medical treatment and self-care. Even with a perfectly tailored medication regimen, lifestyle factors like sleep, nutrition, and exercise play a crucial role in regulating the brain's neurochemistry and building resilience against hormonal ebbs and flows.

For example, a woman may find that during the low-estrogen luteal phase, when her medication feels less effective, she needs to double down on her self-care practices. This could include:

- **Prioritizing Sleep Hygiene:** As quality sleep is critical for attention, emotional control, and working memory, she might need to be even more diligent about her sleep routine during this time, creating a relaxing ritual and avoiding stimulating activities that can trigger insomnia or restlessness.

- **Increasing Physical Activity:** Regular physical exercise can serve as a powerful antidote to mental fatigue, helping to regulate dopamine levels, reduce restlessness, and improve mood, all of which are a significant challenge during the luteal phase.
- **Focusing on Brain-Supporting Nutrition:** A diet rich in omega-3 fatty acids, antioxidants, and protein can help support brain function and stabilize mood and energy levels, providing a buffer against the cognitive and emotional rollercoasters that accompany hormonal shifts.

Furthermore, many women with ADHD have a tendency to internalize their struggles and blame themselves for their difficulties, which can lead to a significant lack of confidence and a sense of being perpetually overwhelmed. It is important to note that stimulant medications enhance the dopamine system and improve executive function.

For this reason, stimulants can be effective in menopausal women, but combining them with non-medication strategies like cognitive-behavioral therapy, coaching, stress management, and exercise can help support executive function, mood, and cognitive health. This integrated approach acknowledges that a woman's well-being is a complex interplay of biology, lifestyle, and psychology.

The link between hormones and ADHD has provided a groundbreaking discussion that validates the lived experience of countless women who have anecdotally reported that their symptoms are profoundly impacted by their hormonal cycles.

By understanding the neurochemical connection, navigating the challenges of the menstrual cycle and menopause, and exploring tailored treatment and self-care strategies, a woman can move from feeling powerless against her symptoms to a place of informed action. This holistic approach ensures that her treatment plan is not a static prescription but a dynamic, lifelong process that accounts for her unique neurobiological needs. This understanding is a crucial step towards achieving genuine balance and well-being.

CHAPTER 5:

HORMONAL SELF-CARE

Beyond medication, a woman can also implement proactive lifestyle strategies to help manage the cognitive and emotional symptoms that arise from hormonal fluctuations. A holistic approach that supports both the brain and the body is essential for building resilience. Regular physical exercise is a powerful tool, as it helps regulate mood and brain function, reduces stress, and improves sleep quality. Good sleep hygiene is also a critical component, as sleep is vital for attention, emotional control, and working memory, and a lack of it can exacerbate hormonal imbalances and ADHD symptoms.

Nutrition plays a significant role in brain health and mood stability. The consumption of foods rich in omega-3 fatty acids, antioxidants, and protein can help support brain function and stabilize mood and energy levels.

A conscious effort to reduce sugars and processed foods can also help to prevent the energy crashes that exacerbate ADHD symptoms. Finally, managing stress through mindfulness and other techniques is crucial, as high stress levels can further disrupt hormonal balance and cognitive function.

By consistently engaging in these self-care strategies, a woman can build a buffer against the hormonal ebbs and flows and create a more stable and supportive internal environment for her ADHD brain.

The Proactive Power of Physical Activity

For a woman with ADHD, regular physical exercise is not just a tool for physical health; it is a profound and proactive strategy for managing the neurochemical and hormonal imbalances that fuel her symptoms.

Research has shown that physical activity has a beneficial effect on inhibitory control in adults with ADHD, a core executive function that helps with impulse control and emotional regulation. It can also improve cognitive function, emotional state, mental health, and physical fitness indicators.

The mechanism behind this is linked to exercise-induced dopamine release, which is associated with improved attention and can help regulate the brain's reward system, which is often dysregulated in individuals with ADHD. Furthermore, exercise can enhance brain plasticity and improve blood flow to the brain, which supports memory and learning.

To make exercise a consistent part of your routine, it's essential to find an activity that is genuinely enjoyable, as the ADHD brain craves novelty and can struggle with boring, repetitive tasks.

This could be dancing, running, swimming, lifting weights, or a team sport. Research suggests that while all forms of physical activity can be beneficial, interventions that involve higher levels of cognitive engagement and motor skill development, such as cognitively enriched aerobic exercise (combining physical activity with simultaneous cognitive tasks), may lead to greater improvements in working memory performance.

Beyond long-term, consistent activity, acute, intense bursts of exercise can also serve as a powerful "brain break" to combat restlessness and re-energize your focus. A brisk walk, a short jog, or a burst of jumping jacks can help to discharge pent-up emotional energy, which is especially useful for a brain prone to emotional dysregulation. This physical "reset button" can prevent an emotional storm from spiraling out of control, as it provides a direct, healthy outlet for intense feelings like anger, anxiety, or frustration.

Prioritizing Sleep Hygiene: The Foundation of Well-Being

Quality sleep is non-negotiable for anyone seeking to maintain optimal cognitive and emotional health, but for a woman with ADHD, it is the bedrock of sustained focus, emotional control, and working memory. Research indicates that an estimated 50-75% of adults with ADHD experience sleeping problems, with studies showing that sleep deprivation in ADHD can be as impairing as other adult symptoms combined.

These sleep challenges often vary by ADHD subtype, with women who have predominantly inattentive symptoms being more likely to have a later bedtime, and those with hyperactive-impulsive symptoms more likely to experience insomnia.

To combat this, a woman must prioritize consistent and healthy sleep hygiene practices. The human body thrives on regularity, and the ADHD brain is no exception. A consistent bedtime and wake-up time, even on weekends, helps regulate your natural sleep rhythm and reinforces the connection between bed and sleep.

- **Create a Relaxing Ritual:** Your bedtime routine should signal to your body that it's time to wind down. This could include listening to a relaxing audiobook, reading a physical book (as opposed to an overstimulating screen), taking a warm bath or shower, or practicing deep breathing exercises. This ritual helps to transition the ADHD brain from its "on the go" state to a calmer state, preparing it for rest.

- **Avoid Stimulating Activities:** In the hours before bed, it is crucial to avoid screens, caffeine, sugar, and stimulating work projects that can trigger hyperfocus. The blue light from screens can interfere with melatonin production, while engaging in a highly stimulating task can make it difficult for the ADHD brain to wind down.

- **Clear Your Mental Clutter:** A racing mind and ruminating on a to-do list or worrying about unfinished tasks can keep you awake. A simple but effective strategy is to take time before bed to write out your "to-do" list for the next day, which helps to offload these worries from your mind, allowing you to relax and fall asleep more easily.

Nourishing Your Brain: Diet and Hydration

What you consume directly impacts your brain's ability to function. Consistent, high-quality fuel is crucial for maintaining stable energy levels, which in turn supports sustained focus and emotional regulation. Dehydration and erratic blood sugar levels can mimic or exacerbate ADHD symptoms, making it even more challenging to stay on track.

- **Mindful Eating:** Focusing on balanced meals with lean protein, healthy fats, and complex carbohydrates is key to maintaining steady energy levels throughout the day. Conversely, a conscious effort to reduce sugars and processed foods can help to prevent the rapid energy spikes followed by a crash that leaves you feeling sluggish and unfocused, which can exacerbate ADHD symptoms.

- **The Power of Omega-3s:** The brain uses omega-3 fatty acids as a building block for cell membranes and as a tool to help neurotransmitters carry signals more effectively. Several studies have linked low omega-3 fatty acid levels to common ADHD symptoms like learning difficulties, hyperactivity, and problems with emotional regulation. Research has shown that supplementing with omega-3s can improve mood, reduce hyperactivity, and even enhance working memory. Fish high in omega-3 fatty acids include mackerel, lake trout, herring, sardines, and salmon.

- **Consistent Hydration:** Staying properly hydrated is essential for optimal brain function and mental clarity. Keeping a water bottle with you and aiming for consistent intake throughout the day can have a significant impact on your focus and mental energy.

Managing Stress: Building a Buffer Against Hormonal Chaos

For a woman with ADHD, the constant effort to manage symptoms, navigate societal expectations, and deal with the relentless demands of daily life can be a source of chronic, low-grade stress.

This prolonged stress can further disrupt hormonal balance and cognitive function. Research shows that high stress levels can worsen working memory deficits and emotional regulation, creating a vicious cycle where ADHD symptoms lead to stress, and stress, in turn, exacerbates ADHD symptoms.

Managing stress is crucial for building resilience against the hormonal ebbs and flows of a woman's life. Mindfulness and other stress-reduction techniques provide the internal toolkit to manage the physiological arousal that comes with stress.

- **Mindfulness Practices:** Mindfulness, such as meditation, journaling, or yoga, can help to support emotional regulation, improve focus, and reduce stress by providing a much-needed anchor for a racing mind. By consistently practicing mindfulness, a woman can learn to become a curious observer of her thoughts and emotions rather than being solely subject to their whims.

- **Deep Breathing Exercises:** When stress levels are high, deep breathing exercises can directly impact your nervous system, promoting a sense of calm and control amidst the chaos. By slowing your breath, you can calm your body's "fight or flight" response and engage its more relaxed, parasympathetic state.

- **Creative Outlets:** Engaging in creative activities such as painting, drawing, or writing can provide a positive outlet for expression and help channel any overwhelming thoughts or emotions, a key skill taught in Dialectical Behavior Therapy (DBT).

By consistently engaging in these self-care strategies, a woman can build a buffer against the hormonal ebbs and flows and create a more stable and supportive internal environment for her ADHD brain. This integrated approach ensures that your newfound capacity for concentration is not only powerful but also sustainable, helping you thrive in a world that constantly vies for your attention, rather than merely survive it.

Conclusion: A Holistic Approach to Hormonal Harmony

This book has provided a groundbreaking discussion on the critical, yet understudied, link between hormones and ADHD in women. It has validated the lived experience of countless women who have anecdotally reported that their symptoms are profoundly impacted by their hormonal cycles.

By understanding the neurochemical connection, navigating the challenges of the menstrual cycle and menopause, and exploring tailored treatment and self-care strategies, a woman can move from feeling powerless against her symptoms to a place of informed action. This holistic approach ensures that her treatment plan is not a static prescription but a dynamic, lifelong process that accounts for her unique neurobiological needs. This understanding is a crucial step towards achieving genuine balance and well-being.

The Liberation of a Scientific Explanation

For too long, the unique challenges of ADHD in women have been overlooked, a reality underscored by a history of male-centric research and diagnostic criteria that fail to capture the nuances of female symptom presentation.

A woman's emotional and cognitive struggles, which are often exacerbated by hormonal shifts, have been dismissed as anxiety, depression, or a mood disorder, leading to misdiagnosis, ineffective treatment, and a profound sense of not being "believed" by the medical community. For many, this lack of validation has fueled a deep and pervasive sense of shame, a feeling that their struggles are a personal failing rather than a neurobiological reality.

This book provides a critical intervention by shining a light on the science behind these struggles. The knowledge that the ebb and flow of estrogen and progesterone are directly linked to the brain's dopamine system is profoundly liberating. It transforms a vague, frustrating feeling of being out of control into a clear, scientific understanding.

You now know that when your symptoms worsen in the days leading up to your period, it's not because you're "moody" or "overly emotional" but because lower levels of estrogen are linked to lower levels of dopamine, which can exacerbate core ADHD challenges. This understanding allows for a powerful shift in perspective, moving from a place of self-blame and frustration to a place of self-compassion and informed action.

The Three Pillars of Hormonal Self-Mastery

The holistic approach to hormonal harmony presented in this book is built on three core pillars: understanding the neurobiology, tracking your unique patterns, and implementing tailored, proactive strategies. This is a dynamic process that recognizes a woman's hormonal journey as a constant, ever-changing landscape, not a static condition.

1. Understanding the Neurobiological Landscape: You have learned that ADHD is not a static condition but a dynamic experience that changes across a woman's lifespan in concert with her hormonal journey.

- **The Menstrual Cycle:** You now understand that the low-estrogen, high-progesterone environment of the luteal phase, which precedes menstruation, can intensify symptoms of inattention, anxiety, and emotional dysregulation. This is why many women anecdotally report that their attention is better before ovulation and can worsen after. This insight is a powerful tool for self-compassion, as it provides a clear, non-judgmental explanation for a woman's fluctuating capacity for focus and emotional control throughout the month. The knowledge of this link is a crucial step toward managing the intense mood swings, irritability, and anger associated with the co-occurrence of ADHD and Premenstrual Dysphoric Disorder (PMDD) that many women report.

- **Perimenopause and Menopause:** You have also gained a deeper understanding of the significant and often unexpected challenge that the hormonal shifts of midlife can present. As estrogen and progesterone levels decline, underlying ADHD symptoms that a woman may have compensated for throughout her life can become unmanageable. This hormonal decline can "unmask" a previously undiagnosed ADHD condition or significantly worsen the symptoms of a diagnosed one, creating what some experts refer to as an "ADHD squared" effect—the compounding of low estrogen and low dopamine. This understanding is crucial for a woman to be able to differentiate between menopausal "brain fog" and a worsening of her ADHD symptoms, providing a clear pathway toward seeking effective support.

2. Becoming a Self-Advocate Through Symptom Tracking: The most powerful tool for navigating this journey is becoming an expert on your own body and mind. For years, women who reported a link between their menstrual cycle and ADHD symptoms were often told by doctors that they "had never heard of anything like that". This profound lack of understanding and belief from the medical community can leave a woman feeling invalidated and hopeless. To move past this, a woman must become an expert on her own body and mind, gathering concrete, objective data to back up her subjective experience.

By diligently tracking her symptoms, a woman can transform her experience from a collection of vague feelings into a clear, visual, and measurable pattern that can be presented to a doctor.

This process turns a subjective report of "I'm more tired and irritable" into an objective report of "My inattention, anxiety, and fatigue scores were consistently 40% higher during the five days leading up to my period for the last three months, and my medication's effectiveness was reduced by 50% during that time." With this data in hand, a woman is in a powerful position to advocate for a more personalized treatment plan, validating her experience and empowering her to take control of her health.

3. Implementing a Tailored, Holistic Treatment Plan: The conversation around medication efficacy and hormones is not just about dosage adjustments; it's about a holistic approach that recognizes the synergy between medical treatment and self-care.

- **Medication and "Cycle Dosing":** The link between hormones and ADHD has led to the development of potential new approaches to treatment, such as "cycle dosing," where medication dosages are tailored to a woman's hormonal status. While research in this area is still limited and in its early stages, it empowers a woman to have a more informed discussion with her doctor about how medication can be a dynamic, rather than static, part of her treatment plan.

- **Proactive Lifestyle Strategies:** Even with a perfectly tailored medication regimen, lifestyle factors like sleep, nutrition, and exercise play a crucial role in regulating the brain's neurochemistry and building resilience against hormonal ebbs and flows. A woman may find that during the low-estrogen luteal phase, when her medication feels less effective, she needs to double down on her self-care practices. This could include prioritizing good sleep hygiene, as quality sleep is critical for attention, emotional control, and working memory. Regular physical exercise can serve as a powerful antidote to mental fatigue, helping to regulate dopamine levels, reduce restlessness, and improve mood. A diet rich in omega-3 fatty acids, antioxidants, and protein can also help support brain function and stabilize mood and energy levels, providing a buffer against the cognitive and emotional rollercoasters that accompany hormonal shifts. Finally, managing stress through mindfulness and other techniques is crucial, as high stress levels can further disrupt hormonal balance and cognitive function.

The Bridge to Your Balanced Life

The work you have done in this book is foundational. A brain that is constantly battling the unpredictable shifts of a hormonal cycle is a brain that has less mental and emotional bandwidth for all the other challenges of living with ADHD. The harmony you have cultivated here is the prerequisite for the more complex work that follows.

- **A Foundation for Emotional Mastery (Book 4):** Emotional dysregulation is a core challenge for women with ADHD, and it is profoundly impacted by hormonal fluctuations. The knowledge you have gained in this book empowers you to recognize that your intense emotional reactions are often a neurobiological reality, not a personal failing. A more stable hormonal baseline provides a woman with more emotional resilience and greater capacity to apply the CBT and DBT tools for emotional regulation that will be explored in the next book. You will be better equipped to manage the intense feelings and emotional dysregulation that are so prevalent in ADHD, and less likely to feel overwhelmed by the minor inconveniences that can trigger a disproportionate emotional storm.

- **A Catalyst for Nurturing Relationships (Book 5):** The unpredictable emotional and cognitive challenges that accompany hormonal shifts can be a significant source of friction in relationships, as a woman's partner may struggle to understand her fluctuating moods or energy levels. By understanding her unique neurobiological needs, a woman is better equipped to communicate them to her loved ones, fostering empathy and understanding. A more stable internal environment, achieved through hormonal harmony, provides a more predictable and reliable emotional base for building and sustaining meaningful relationships.

By consistently engaging in these self-care strategies, a woman can build a buffer against the hormonal ebbs and flows and create a more stable and supportive internal environment for her ADHD brain. This integrated approach ensures that her treatment plan is not a static prescription but a dynamic, lifelong process that accounts for her unique neurobiological needs. This understanding is a crucial step towards achieving genuine balance and well-being, and is the essential foundation for the rest of your journey.

Reflection questions

- The book validates the link between hormonal fluctuations and ADHD symptoms. How has understanding this connection helped you to be more compassionate with yourself during different phases of your hormonal cycle?
- What is one lifestyle strategy (e.g., exercise, nutrition, sleep) that you can implement to support your brain's neurochemistry and build resilience against hormonal shifts?

- The text discusses a "holistic approach" to treatment. What is one new piece of information you can share with your healthcare professional to advocate for a more personalized treatment plan?

BOOK FOUR:

MASTER YOUR EMOTIONS:

A PRACTICAL TOOLKIT FOR THE ADHD WOMAN

INTRODUCTION:

THE EMOTIONAL ROLLERCOASTER AND THE QUEST FOR REGULATION

For many women with ADHD, the journey of self-mastery is often defined by the profound challenge of emotional regulation. While a woman may be highly capable and intelligent, an intense emotional surge, a flash of anger, a wave of anxiety, or the crushing sting of a perceived criticism, can feel impossible to control, derailing her best intentions and leaving a wake of regret.

This isn't a character flaw or a sign of being overly sensitive; it is a core, significant, and often misunderstood aspect of ADHD. Research consistently shows that emotional dysregulation, or the difficulty in managing and appropriately expressing emotions, is a prominent feature of the disorder.

For women, this can manifest differently than in men, often leading to a greater tendency to internalize feelings and blame themselves for their struggles, a pattern that fuels anxiety, depression, and a shattered sense of self-worth. This book will provide a compassionate, evidence-based roadmap to help a woman navigate this inner emotional landscape.

The Neurobiological Underpinnings of Emotional Dysregulation

The emotional dysregulation experienced by women with ADHD is a genuine, neurobiological reality, not a personal failing. Research suggests that a key factor is the distinct functioning and structure of the ADHD brain, particularly in areas responsible for emotional processing and regulation. While the traditional narrative of ADHD has focused on inattention and hyperactivity, the experience of intense, unpredictable emotions is one of the most debilitating and pervasive symptoms for many women.

At the center of this challenge is a disconnect between the brain's emotional center and its "command center" for self-control. The amygdala, a small, almond-shaped region deep within the brain, is the brain's alarm system, responsible for detecting and responding to threats, and it often has an overactive response in individuals with ADHD, leading to a quick trigger for strong emotions like anger, fear, and frustration.

The frontal cortex, which is responsible for higher-level executive functions, acts as the brain's "brakes," allowing you to pause, think, and inhibit an automatic reaction before it takes over. Studies have shown a decreased activation of the frontal cortex in the ADHD brain, making it less likely to inhibit big reactions as it's supposed to. This means there is a disconnect between the emotional accelerator and the emotional brakes, leading to a profound difficulty in controlling and regulating the intensity and duration of feelings.

This struggle is further complicated by the dysregulation of key neurotransmitters, such as dopamine, which is heavily involved in the brain's motivation, reward, and mood systems. When dopamine levels are inconsistent, a woman may struggle with emotional regulation and experience mood swings that are hard to predict, leaving her feeling frenzied, frazzled, and overwhelmed. The combination of a less active frontal cortex and a dysregulated neurochemical system creates a perfect storm for emotional dysregulation, where emotions can feel "all or nothing," and even minor inconveniences can trigger an overwhelming emotional response.

The Nuances of Emotional Dysregulation in Women

While emotional dysregulation is a prominent feature of ADHD regardless of gender, its manifestation and consequences can be dramatically different for women. The pressure of societal expectations for women to be emotionally mature, nurturing, and calm creates a direct conflict with the core symptoms of ADHD, forcing many women to internalize their struggles and blame themselves for their difficulties. This internalization is often a stark contrast to men, who are more likely to externalize their frustration through anger and defensiveness.

For a woman with ADHD, this internalization can take several forms:

- **Intense Emotional Surges:** Emotions can flare up with startling speed and intensity. A minor inconvenience can lead to a disproportionate outburst, or a small disappointment can trigger a deep, overwhelming wave of sadness. This isn't simply about being moody; it's a genuine difficulty in modulating the intensity, duration, and even the type of emotional response.

- **A Low Tolerance for Frustration:** A hallmark of this dysregulation is a low tolerance for frustrating situations. The immense, amorphous nature of tasks, coupled with the internal restlessness of the ADHD brain, can lead a woman to feel so overwhelmed that she gives up on a project before she even starts, leading to a cycle of self-blame and avoidance.

- **Pervasive Feelings of Overwhelm and Fatigue:** The constant, conscious effort to manage internalized symptoms—such as a racing mind and emotional dysregulation—that neurotypical individuals do unconsciously is a significant drain on mental energy. This constant cognitive effort is the "ADHD tax" that depletes mental energy reserves and makes a woman more susceptible to burnout, leading to a chronic sense of being "frenzied, frazzled, and overwhelmed".

Rejection Sensitive Dysphoria (RSD): A Deeper Look

A particularly painful and debilitating manifestation of emotional dysregulation that is highly common in women with ADHD is Rejection Sensitive Dysphoria (RSD). While not a formal medical diagnosis, RSD is a descriptive term for an "extreme emotional responsiveness and anxiety in anticipation of, or in response to, perceived rejection or criticism from others". For a woman with ADHD, this is more than just feeling hurt; it is an immediate, overwhelming emotional pain that can feel physically agonizing, sometimes described as akin to being punched in the gut or stabbed in the heart.

This profound hypersensitivity is fueled by a lifetime of internalizing struggles and the fear that their "perceived failures" will be discovered. For many women, their resilience was chipped away by early traumatic experiences of chronic negative feedback, bullying, exclusion, and humiliation from family, peers, and teachers. This repeated threat of rejection can trigger primitive survival mechanisms, often causing a woman to "freeze up" or become unable to act. This sets the stage for a learned expectation of future social adversity and a deep-seated fear that they are, in fact, unworthy of love and acceptance.

The pain of RSD is often amplified by the fact that women with ADHD are more prone to internalizing their struggles, interpreting this painful experience as a personal failing that confirms a deeply held belief of inadequacy. A woman's emotional volatility may be seen as a "melodramatic overreaction" by others, which further invalidates her pain and reinforces her sense of being unworthy.

This painful feedback loop, where emotional dysregulation leads to RSD, and RSD feeds a deep sense of shame, creates a devastating barrier to authentic connection and self-acceptance. This shame, when left unaddressed, can lead to dangerous behaviors, including self-harm and suicidal thoughts, at a much greater rate than in their male counterparts. To cope, a woman may become a people-pleaser or a perfectionist to avoid any potential criticism, a strategy that is both exhausting and unsustainable.

The Impact on Mental Health and Relationships

The collective toll of this emotional rollercoaster is significant and often leads to a variety of co-occurring conditions and challenges that further destabilize a woman's life. Research confirms that a repeated pattern of failures and frustrations due to ADHD can contribute to or worsen other mental health conditions, such as depression and anxiety, which are highly prevalent in women with ADHD.

In fact, many women are initially diagnosed with anxiety or a mood disorder before the underlying ADHD is identified, leading to a long and frustrating journey of ineffective treatment. The sadness and shame that arise from the feelings of "never fitting in" to social groups is a major part of the lived experience of women with ADHD.

These emotional struggles also have a profound impact on relationships. For a woman with ADHD, difficulty with emotional regulation can make it hard to respond to a partner's frustrations calmly, leading to disagreements that spiral out of control. Her impulsive emotional reactions can lead to her saying things she later regrets, which can cause significant friction and misunderstanding. Furthermore, a woman with ADHD may struggle to read social cues, and her tendency to over-talk or interrupt in conversation can make it difficult for her to form and maintain friendships, leading to feelings of loneliness and isolation.

The emotional volatility, combined with the other challenges of ADHD, often leads to a sense of inadequacy and self-blame, a pattern that is significantly more prevalent in women with ADHD than in men. This book provides a much-needed roadmap for navigating this inner landscape, moving a woman from a place of emotional reactivity to one of thoughtful, intentional response.

A Compassionate, Evidence-Based Roadmap for Emotional Mastery

The journey to emotional mastery for a woman with ADHD is not about suppressing your emotions or pretending they don't exist; it is about developing a guiding hand to lead you through your inner world with greater awareness and control. The solution lies in building a robust, evidence-based toolkit that acknowledges your neurobiological reality while providing a strategic pathway toward self-regulation.

This book will provide a comprehensive roadmap to navigate this inner emotional landscape, drawing on the principles of Cognitive Behavioral Therapy (CBT) and Dialectical Behavioral Therapy (DBT), which are highly effective therapeutic approaches for managing the emotional dysregulation, anxiety, and stress that frequently co-occur with ADHD. These tools will empower a woman to develop a keen awareness of her emotional triggers, understand the intricate connection between her thoughts, feelings, and actions, and build a robust toolkit to respond to emotions more effectively and constructively.

We will begin by providing a framework for identifying and challenging the distorted thoughts that often fuel intense emotional reactions, which is a cornerstone of CBT. We will then delve into practical behavioral strategies from DBT, such as mindful movement, sensory grounding, and the "STOP" skill, which provide direct, actionable steps to either reduce the immediate intensity of an emotion or shift your physiological and psychological state to a more regulated one.

This will be followed by a discussion on how to build emotional resilience and distress tolerance, equipping you with the capacity to endure and cope with uncomfortable emotional states without resorting to impulsive, unhelpful behaviors. Finally, we will explore the critical role of compassionate self-talk in transforming your inner critic into an inner ally who supports your growth, resilience, and emotional well-being, which is an essential antidote to the shame that so many women with ADHD feel.

This compassionate, evidence-based roadmap is designed to empower a woman to transform her relationship with her emotions, moving from a place of chronic emotional turbulence to one of intentional, thoughtful response. This mastery of her inner world is the bedrock upon which all other areas of her life, from relationships to productivity, are built, and it is a crucial step towards achieving genuine balance and well-being.

CHAPTER 1:

EMOTIONAL DYSREGULATION

Emotional dysregulation in women with ADHD is a nuanced and pervasive struggle. It is marked by a heightened emotional intensity and a surprising lack of an internal "buffer" or "brakes" to modulate feelings. This can lead to emotions that feel all-or-nothing, where a woman might hold back her feelings to fit in, but a small trigger can unleash an overwhelming emotional response.

Research suggests that this is due to differences in brain function, particularly in the frontal cortex, which is less likely to inhibit big reactions. This often manifests as rapidly shifting moods and a low tolerance for frustration, where minor inconveniences can trigger a disproportionate emotional storm.

A woman may go from calm to intensely frustrated or angry in moments, followed by feelings of deep sadness or shame over her reaction. Unlike their male counterparts who may be more likely to externalize their frustration through anger, women are more prone to internalizing their struggles, leading to self-blame, anxiety, depression, and low self-esteem.

The Neurobiology of the Emotional Brain

The emotional dysregulation experienced by women with ADHD is not a character flaw or a sign of being overly sensitive; it is a core, significant, and often misunderstood aspect of ADHD that is rooted in neurobiological differences. While the traditional narrative of ADHD has focused on inattention and hyperactivity, a growing body of contemporary research highlights that emotional dysregulation is a pervasive and often debilitating aspect of the disorder.

At the center of this challenge is a disconnect between the brain's emotional centers and its "command center" for self-control. The amygdala, a small, almond-shaped region deep within the brain, is the brain's alarm system, responsible for detecting and responding to threats. In individuals with ADHD, this alarm system can be overactive, leading to a quick trigger for strong emotions like anger, fear, and frustration.

The frontal cortex, which is responsible for higher-level executive functions, acts as the brain's "brakes," allowing you to pause, think, and inhibit an automatic reaction before it takes over. Research has found that there is a decreased activation of the frontal cortex in the ADHD brain, making it less likely to inhibit these big reactions as it's supposed to. This means there is a disconnect between the emotional accelerator and the emotional brakes, leading to a profound difficulty in controlling and regulating the intensity and duration of feelings.

This struggle is further complicated by the dysregulation of key neurotransmitters, such as dopamine, which is heavily involved in the brain's motivation, reward, and mood systems. When dopamine levels are inconsistent, a woman may struggle with emotional regulation and experience mood swings that are hard to predict, leaving her feeling "frenzied, frazzled, and overwhelmed".

The combination of a less active frontal cortex and a dysregulated neurochemical system creates a perfect storm for emotional dysregulation, where emotions can feel "all or nothing," and even minor inconveniences can trigger an overwhelming emotional response.

The Nuances of Emotional Dysregulation in Women

While emotional dysregulation is a prominent feature of ADHD regardless of gender, its manifestation and consequences can be dramatically different for women. The pressure of societal expectations for women to be emotionally mature, nurturing, and calm creates a direct conflict with the core symptoms of ADHD, forcing many women to internalize their struggles and blame themselves for their difficulties.

This internalization is often in stark contrast to men, who are more likely to externalize their frustration through anger and defensiveness, leading to a diagnostic disparity where girls' and women's symptoms are often overlooked or misdiagnosed as a mood disorder.

For a woman with ADHD, internalization can take several forms:

- **Intense Emotional Surges:** Emotions can flare up with startling speed and intensity. A minor inconvenience can lead to a disproportionate outburst, or a small disappointment can trigger a deep, overwhelming wave of sadness that feels all-consuming. This is not simply about being moody; it's a genuine difficulty in modulating the intensity, duration, and even the type of emotional response.

- **Low Tolerance for Frustration:** A hallmark of this dysregulation is a low tolerance for frustrating situations. The immense, amorphous nature of tasks, coupled with the internal restlessness of the ADHD brain, can lead a woman to feel so overwhelmed that she gives up on a project before she even starts, leading to a cycle of self-blame and avoidance. The emotional distress that arises from these challenges can be so severe that it contributes to or worsens co-occurring mental health conditions like anxiety and depression.

- **Pervasive Feelings of Overwhelm and Fatigue:** The constant, conscious effort to manage internalized symptoms, such as a racing mind and emotional dysregulation, that neurotypical individuals do unconsciously is a significant drain on mental energy. This constant cognitive effort is the "ADHD tax" that depletes mental energy reserves and makes a woman more susceptible to burnout, a state of chronic exhaustion that research shows is significantly higher in employees with ADHD due to executive function difficulties. A woman might report feeling perpetually "frenzied, frazzled, and overwhelmed".

The Pervasive Toll of Internalization and Masking

A particularly painful and debilitating manifestation of emotional dysregulation is Rejection Sensitive Dysphoria (RSD), a common experience among women with ADHD that involves an extreme emotional responsiveness to perceived rejection or criticism. For a woman with ADHD, this is more than just feeling hurt; it is an immediate, overwhelming emotional pain that can feel physically agonizing, sometimes described as akin to being punched in the gut.

This hypersensitivity is fueled by a lifetime of internalizing struggles and the fear that their "perceived failures" will be discovered and provoke rejection.

For many women, their resilience was chipped away by early traumatic experiences of chronic negative feedback, bullying, and humiliation from family, peers, and teachers. This painful experience is often interpreted as a personal failing, confirming a deeply held belief of inadequacy that can be a major part of the lived experience of women with ADHD.

This cycle of emotional dysregulation leading to RSD, and RSD feeding shame, creates a devastating barrier to authentic connection and self-acceptance. This shame, when left unaddressed, can lead to dangerous behaviors, including self-harm and suicidal thoughts, at a much greater rate than in their male counterparts.

Emotional volatility is often made worse by the practice of "masking," where women develop sophisticated compensatory behaviors to hide their struggles and appear "neurotypical" to the outside world. While this may be a survival strategy developed to avoid social rejection, it can also lead to chronic loneliness and a debilitating sense of not being able to be one's authentic self. A woman might meticulously maintain a façade of punctuality, or she might learn to pretend to take notes in a meeting to hide the fact that she is "zoning out" or has a "thousand-yard stare".

The stress of this constant, exhausting effort to appear "non-ADHD" is an invisible burden that leads to a lifetime of internalized shame, anxiety, depression, and a shattered sense of self-worth. Studies confirm that girls are more likely to mask their symptoms than boys, and this can lead to significant negative consequences on their mental health, social functioning, and academic achievement.

The Cycle of Emotional Dysregulation and Mental Health

The collective toll of this emotional rollercoaster is significant and often leads to a variety of co-occurring conditions that further destabilize a woman's life. Research confirms that a repeated pattern of failures and frustrations due to ADHD can contribute to or worsen other mental health conditions, such as depression and anxiety, which are highly prevalent in women with ADHD.

In fact, a woman may be diagnosed with anxiety, depression, or a mood disorder before the underlying ADHD is identified, leading to a long and frustrating journey of ineffective treatment. A new assessment, BRIEF2A, even divides executive function deficits into behavioral regulation, emotional regulation, and cognitive regulation, highlighting the importance of understanding this interplay in a clinical setting.

Furthermore, the intersection of ADHD and Premenstrual Dysphoric Disorder (PMDD) is highly significant, with over 40% of women with ADHD also experiencing PMDD, a more severe form of PMS. The combination of these two conditions can make emotional regulation even more challenging, leading to more pronounced mood swings, irritability, and anger.

This is because PMDD, like ADHD, is linked to changes in the brain and hormones, and the combination can create a perfect storm of emotional dysregulation that is difficult to manage without a holistic approach.

The path forward, therefore, is not to simply suppress these emotions or pretend they don't exist. It's about developing a guiding hand to lead you through your inner world with greater awareness and control. The solution lies in building a robust, evidence-based toolkit that acknowledges your neurobiological reality while providing a strategic pathway toward self-regulation.

This book will provide a compassionate, evidence-based roadmap to help a woman navigate this inner emotional landscape, drawing on the principles of Cognitive Behavioral Therapy (CBT) and Dialectical Behavioral Therapy (DBT), which are highly effective therapeutic approaches for managing the emotional dysregulation, anxiety, and stress that frequently co-occur with ADHD. These tools will empower a woman to develop a keen awareness of her emotional triggers, understand the intricate connection between her thoughts, feelings, and actions, and build a robust toolkit to respond to emotions more effectively and constructively.

The journey to emotional mastery for a woman with ADHD is not about becoming emotionless or suppressing who you are, but about developing the capacity to respond to life's inevitable challenges with greater intention, resilience, and effectiveness. This mastery of her inner world is the bedrock upon which all other areas of her life, from relationships to productivity, are built, and it is a crucial step towards achieving genuine balance and well-being.

CHAPTER 2:

REJECTION SENSITIVE DYSPHORIA (RSD)

A particularly painful and debilitating manifestation of emotional dysregulation is Rejection Sensitive Dysphoria (RSD), a common experience among women with ADHD that involves an extreme emotional responsiveness to perceived rejection or criticism. For a woman with ADHD, this is more than just feeling hurt; it is an immediate, overwhelming emotional pain that can feel physically agonizing. This pain is often triggered not by actual rejection, but by a perceived snub, a tone of voice, or a hint of disapproval.

This hypersensitivity is fueled by a lifetime of internalizing struggles and the fear that their "perceived failures" will be discovered, a fear that can lead a woman to become a perfectionist or a people-pleaser to avoid any potential criticism.

Such a painful feedback loop is amplified by the fact that women are more likely to internalize their struggles. This painful experience is often interpreted as a personal failing, confirming a deeply held belief of inadequacy. A woman's emotional volatility may be seen as a "melodramatic overreaction" by others, which further invalidates her pain and reinforces her sense of being unworthy. This cycle of emotional dysregulation leading to RSD, and RSD feeding shame, creates a devastating barrier to authentic connection and self-acceptance.

The Neurobiology of Rejection Pain

While RSD is not a formal diagnosis or disorder in official medical manuals, its profound impact on a woman's quality of life is undeniable, and research is beginning to uncover the neurobiological roots of this intense experience. Experts believe that the extreme emotional pain that defines RSD, the feeling of being punched in the gut or stabbed in the heart, is a real, physiological response in the ADHD brain. This intense, overwhelming pain is what separates RSD from basic emotional dysregulation.

The underlying mechanism is thought to involve a distinct functioning of brain regions responsible for emotional processing and regulation, particularly the amygdala and the prefrontal cortex. The amygdala acts as the brain's alarm system, and in individuals with ADHD, this system can be overactive, leading to a quick trigger for strong emotions like anger, fear, and frustration. When a person with ADHD experiences a perceived rejection, the amygdala's alarm bells may ring with a disproportionate intensity, leading to an immediate and overwhelming emotional response.

At the same time, the prefrontal cortex, which is responsible for the brain's "brakes" and allows for a thoughtful, inhibited response, may be less active in the ADHD brain. This creates a disconnect between the emotional accelerator and the emotional brakes, leading to a profound difficulty in controlling and modulating the intensity of the rejection-based feelings.

This neurological difference explains why a woman may go from calm to intensely frustrated or angry in moments, followed by feelings of deep sadness or shame over her reaction, as the emotional wave hits with little warning and overwhelms her ability to self-regulate.

The Origins of Hypersensitivity: A Lifetime of Negative Feedback

The hypersensitivity of RSD is not a random occurrence; it is often a direct result of a lifetime of chronic negative feedback and a learned expectation of rejection. Research shows that girls and women with ADHD are often met with a lack of understanding from a young age, as their symptoms of disorganization, inattention, and emotional over-reactivity are inconsistent with societal expectations for girls. This can lead to a childhood filled with misunderstanding, self-blame, and rejection from family, peers, and teachers. For example, girls with ADHD may be bullied or ostracized for being overly sensitive or for missing social cues, which sets the stage for a deep-seated fear of social adversity later in life.

A constant stream of criticism and humiliation chips away at a girl's resilience, altering her brain chemistry and increasing her vulnerability to emotional pain. These early traumatic experiences, which are often unpredictable, inescapable, and repeated, can trigger primitive survival mechanisms in the brain. When faced with a threat of rejection, a woman's brain, too vulnerable for a "fight or flight" response, may instead "freeze up," leaving her unable to act.

These episodes of learned helplessness in the face of perceived rejection create a painful feedback loop that reinforces her belief that her behavior merits rejection and that she is, indeed, unworthy. A new assessment, BRIEF2A, even divides executive function deficits into emotional, behavioral, and cognitive regulation, highlighting the importance of understanding this interplay in a clinical setting.

The Social Cost: People-Pleasing and the Impostor Syndrome

This profound hypersensitivity to rejection often drives a woman with ADHD to develop sophisticated compensatory behaviors to avoid any potential criticism. She may become a perfectionist in her work, believing that a flawless performance is the only way to shield herself from judgment.

She may also become a people-pleaser, constantly trying to accommodate the needs of others while neglecting her own, as a way to curry favor and prevent others from seeing her "perceived failures". This strategy, while it may provide temporary emotional safety, is both exhausting and unsustainable.

A constant effort to avoid rejection is often rooted in a deep-seated fear of being discovered as a fraud. For women with ADHD who have successfully "masked" their symptoms for a lifetime, a sense of impostor syndrome is a common companion. They fear that their well-guarded secret, the constant struggle with focus, disorganization, and emotional dysregulation, will be revealed, and that they will finally be rejected for who they truly are. This fear of exposure creates a constant, low-grade anxiety that makes it incredibly difficult to form authentic connections and truly feel accepted.

This painful feedback loop is amplified by the fact that women are more likely to internalize their struggles, a pattern that is often a stark contrast to men, who are more likely to externalize their responses with defensiveness, anger, and projecting blame on others. An internalized experience is often misinterpreted by others, as a woman's emotional volatility may be seen as a "melodramatic overreaction," which further invalidates her pain and reinforces her sense of being unworthy.

A woman's emotional volatility may be seen as a "melodramatic overreaction" by others, which further invalidates her pain and reinforces her sense of being unworthy. This cycle of emotional dysregulation leading to RSD, and RSD feeding shame, creates a devastating barrier to authentic connection and self-acceptance.

The Impact on Relationships and Mental Health

The consequences of unmanaged RSD can be severe and far-reaching, profoundly impacting a woman's mental health and relationships. In romantic relationships, RSD can make it incredibly difficult to navigate conflict and criticism. Even if a partner calmly expresses a concern, the "lens of ADHD" can color their statements as being overtly critical or micromanaging, which triggers an intense emotional reaction and can lead to a spiral of hurt and defensiveness.

It can create a dysfunctional "parent-child" dynamic, where the ADHD partner feels scolded and the neurotypical partner feels frustrated and unheard, leading to a breakdown in communication and a loss of intimacy.

The painful experience of RSD is also strongly linked to mental health struggles. Research shows a significant connection between RSD and feelings of depression, anxiety, and a shattered sense of self-worth. For women with ADHD, who already experience higher rates of anxiety and depression than the general population, the added burden of RSD can be debilitating. Studies reveal that the cumulative effect of a lifetime of negative feedback and a feeling of unworthiness can lead to a significant decline in a woman's mental health, and RSD can be a key factor in driving a woman to self-harm and even suicidal ideation at a much greater rate than her male counterparts. The despair that comes from a belief in their own unworthiness and the constant feeling that they "can do nothing right" can lead to dangerous behaviors, including substance abuse and self-harm.

The link between emotional dysregulation and ADHD is so central that a significant number of women are initially diagnosed with anxiety, depression, or a mood disorder before the underlying ADHD is identified, leading to a long and frustrating journey of ineffective treatment.

This is further complicated by the fact that the intense mood swings, irritability, and anger associated with RSD can overlap with symptoms of Premenstrual Dysphoric Disorder (PMDD), which is disproportionately common in women with ADHD, creating a perfect storm of emotional dysregulation that is difficult to manage without a holistic approach.

The profound impact of RSD is a call for a new approach, one that moves beyond simply validating the pain to providing a concrete roadmap for managing it. This is not about becoming less sensitive or trying to suppress who you are, but about developing a guiding hand to lead you through your inner world with greater awareness and control. The goal is to build a robust, evidence-based toolkit that acknowledges your neurobiological reality while providing a strategic pathway toward self-regulation.

By understanding the origins of your emotional pain, recognizing your triggers, and learning to create a crucial pause between stimulus and response, you can begin to transform your relationship with rejection from a source of profound emotional agony to a manageable, though still difficult, part of your life. This chapter sets the stage for the practical, CBT-based strategies that will empower you to break free from the cycle of shame, people-pleasing, and avoidance that RSD creates, and to build a life of genuine self-acceptance and authentic connection.

CHAPTER 3:

CBT TOOLS: IDENTIFYING AND CHALLENGING UNHELPFUL THOUGHTS

To gain mastery over emotional dysregulation, an essential task is understanding the connection between thoughts, feelings, and behaviors. Cognitive Behavioral Therapy (CBT) is a powerful, evidence-based approach that helps a person identify and challenge unhelpful or irrational thought patterns, which are often at the root of intense emotional reactions.

A crucial first step is recognizing common cognitive distortions that women with ADHD are prone to, such as "catastrophizing", blowing a small mistake into a major disaster, or "mind reading," which involves assuming a negative judgment from others without any evidence.

By learning to pause and question these automatic thoughts, a woman can break the cycle of emotional reactivity. She can ask herself:

"Is that thought 100% true? What is the evidence for it? What is a more balanced way to look at this?" Applied consistently, this process helps a woman reframe her inner narrative from one of self-blame to one of understanding and compassion.

The Foundational Principle of CBT: Thoughts Are Not Facts

The fundamental premise of Cognitive Behavioral Therapy (CBT) is elegantly simple yet profoundly impactful: your thoughts are not facts. Thoughts are interpretations of reality, often automatic and unexamined, and these interpretations directly and powerfully influence how you feel and how you act.

For a woman with ADHD, who may experience rapid shifts in mood and intense emotional responses, these quick, often automatic, and unhelpful thought patterns are particularly impactful, amplifying her emotional rollercoaster. Decades of rigorous research have demonstrated CBT's efficacy in helping individuals identify, evaluate, and ultimately change unhelpful thinking patterns, leading to significant and lasting improvements in mood, anxiety, and stress levels.

Consider a common scenario: receiving an email with critical feedback from a boss. The event itself is neutral; your interpretation of the event dictates your subsequent emotional and behavioral response. A distorted thought pattern, for instance, might be, "I'm a complete failure. I can never do anything right. This proves I'm incompetent, and they're definitely going to fire me for this small mistake".

Such a thought would likely lead to intense shame, crippling anxiety, and despair, causing a woman to procrastinate further on the task, avoid interacting with the boss, and ruminate endlessly on the negative thought, leading to reduced productivity and increased stress.

A balanced, helpful thought, on the other hand, would be, "This feedback is tough to hear. It points out an area where I can improve. What specifically can I learn from this? How can I implement this feedback and improve next time? Everyone makes mistakes." Such a thought would likely lead to feelings of concern and determination, but without the crushing weight of shame. The same external event can lead to vastly different emotional and behavioral outcomes based solely on your initial, often automatic, thought.

The ADHD Brain and its Susceptibility to Distorted Thoughts

Neurobiologically, a woman with ADHD is often more susceptible to these pervasive "thinking traps" or cognitive distortions. The emotional dysregulation so common in women with ADHD is rooted in the distinct functioning and structure of the ADHD brain, particularly in areas responsible for emotional processing and regulation.

The amygdala, the brain's alarm system, is often overactive, leading to a quick trigger for strong emotions like anger, fear, and frustration. Conversely, the frontal cortex, which is responsible for higher-level executive functions and acts as the brain's "brakes," is less likely to inhibit these big reactions, making it difficult to regulate the intensity and duration of feelings.

In this neurobiological context, thoughts can become powerful catalysts for emotional turmoil. A fleeting negative thought, unexamined and unchallenged, can quickly be amplified by an overactive amygdala and an underactive frontal cortex, leading to a full-blown emotional storm.

Furthermore, the challenges of ADHD, such as difficulties with planning, working memory, and consistent follow-through, can create a lifetime of frustrating experiences that reinforce negative self-talk. A woman may be prone to a harsh inner critic, which, as research shows, is a major contributor to shame and feelings of inadequacy in women with ADHD.

Unmasking Common Cognitive Distortions

Cognitive distortions are irrational or exaggerated thought patterns that reinforce negative thinking, undermine self-esteem, and exacerbate emotional distress. They are like mental shortcuts that, while sometimes quick, often lead you down a wrong path. Recognizing them is the first crucial step toward challenging them and reclaiming control over your emotional responses.

- **All-or-Nothing Thinking (Black-and-White Thinking):** Seeing things in extremes, with no middle ground. Everything is either perfect or a total disaster, a complete success or an utter failure. For instance, a woman might think, "I missed that deadline, so I'm a total failure and completely incompetent at my job," discounting all past successes and efforts. A woman might also think, "If I can't do it perfectly, there's no point in starting it at all," which fuels procrastination and perfectionism. This distortion often stems from the ADHD brain's tendency to struggle with nuance and moderation.

- **Catastrophizing:** Exaggerating the negative consequences of an event, jumping to the worst possible conclusion, even when it's highly unlikely. For example, a woman might think, "If I forget to pay this bill today, my credit will be ruined, I'll go bankrupt, and I'll lose everything I own." This distortion is heavily linked to Rejection Sensitive Dysphoria (RSD), where a perceived disapproval from a partner can escalate to thoughts of an impending catastrophe and a relationship ending, turning a minor oversight into an apocalyptic scenario.

- **Mind Reading:** Assuming you know what others are thinking or feeling, usually negatively, without any actual evidence. An example would be, "My boss didn't say hello to me this morning and walked past without a smile, so she must think I'm doing a terrible job and is disappointed in my performance." This distortion is extremely common and painful for women with RSD, as their hypersensitivity to perceived rejection makes them prone to jumping to negative conclusions about others' intentions and feelings towards them.

- **"Should" Statements:** Holding rigid, often unrealistic, expectations for yourself or others, often expressed with words like "should," "must," or "ought." When these expectations are not met, they lead to intense guilt, shame, and frustration. A woman might think, "I should be able to focus for hours without any distractions, just like everyone else," which ignores the neurobiological reality of ADHD. These "shoulds" are often internalized from societal expectations that do not account for neurodiversity and female symptom presentation, leaving women with ADHD particularly vulnerable to feelings of shame and inadequacy.

- **Emotional Reasoning:** Believing something is true solely because you feel it strongly, treating your feelings as definitive evidence of reality. For instance, a woman might think, "I feel like a lazy, unproductive person today, so I must be lazy and incapable," which discounts all her efforts and past accomplishments. The intensity of ADHD emotions can make this distortion particularly compelling and difficult to challenge.

- **Overgeneralization:** Drawing a sweeping negative conclusion based on a single event or piece of evidence, assuming that if something happened once, it will always happen, or that it applies to all situations. An example would be, "I messed up that presentation last week, so I'm terrible at public speaking and will never succeed in any leadership role." This distortion can exacerbate feelings of inadequacy.

- **Personalization:** Blaming yourself for external events or taking things personally that are not actually your fault, or over-attributing events to your own actions. An example would be, "Our team project failed because I didn't push hard enough on my part," even when multiple factors were involved. This distortion can tie into RSD, where any negative outcome is quickly internalized as a personal failing.

- **Disqualifying the Positive:** Ignoring, discounting, or dismissing positive experiences, compliments, or achievements, often by saying they "don't count" or were due to luck. For example, a woman might think, "I finished that tough project ahead of schedule, but anyone could have done it; it was just easy." This distortion sabotages efforts to build self-worth and recognize progress, a key motivator for the ADHD brain.

The Practice: Becoming a Thought Detective

The key to breaking free from the grip of distorted thoughts is to become a detective of your own mind. This is an active process of observation, questioning, and re-framing. When you notice a strong negative emotion, pause and investigate the thoughts that immediately preceded it.

Step 1: Catch the Thought (The "Pause and Observe") When you feel a sudden surge of a strong negative emotion, whether it's anger, shame, intense anxiety, crushing frustration, or deep sadness, use that emotion as a trigger. Ask yourself: "What thought just went through my mind right before I felt this way?" or "What am I telling myself right now about this situation or about myself?" Write the thought down immediately, even if it feels silly or fragmented. The act of externalizing the thought helps you gain some crucial distance from it, allowing you to view it as an object of analysis rather than an undeniable truth. This is the first, most vital step in breaking the automatic emotional reaction.

Step 2: Challenge the Thought (The "Courtroom Test") Once you have identified the thought, put it on trial. Imagine you are a neutral judge or a rigorous lawyer, meticulously examining the evidence for and against the thought.

- **Ask for the evidence:** What is the concrete, factual evidence that this thought is true? What is the evidence against it? Be specific and factual, not just general feelings or past assumptions.

- **Look for alternatives:** Are there other, more balanced ways to interpret the situation? What might a neutral observer see?

- **Name the distortion:** Am I falling into one of the thinking traps or cognitive distortions I just learned about? Naming the distortion helps you to depersonalize it.

- **Practice perspective-taking:** What would I tell a friend in this exact situation if they came to me with this thought? We are often far kinder and more rational with others than we are with ourselves.

- **Assess its helpfulness:** Is this thought helpful? Does it move me towards my goals or away from them? Does it help me feel better or worse? A thought can be partially true but still unhelpful and unproductive.

Step 3: Reframe and Replace (The "Constructive Alternative") Based on your rigorous questioning, formulate a more balanced, realistic, and ultimately more helpful thought. This is not about forced positive affirmations that feel untrue or saccharine; it is about finding a more accurate, nuanced, and empowering perspective that reflects reality more fully.

- **Original Distorted Thought (All-or-Nothing):** "I didn't finish everything on my to-do list today, so today was a complete waste and I'm a failure."
- **Reframed Thought:** "I didn't finish everything, but I did complete, and that's solid progress. It wasn't a perfect day, but it wasn't a total waste. I'll re-prioritize for tomorrow and continue my momentum."
- **Original Distorted Thought (Catastrophizing/RSD):** "My partner looked annoyed when I brought up the chore list; he must be mad at me, and our relationship is in trouble; he'll probably leave me."
- **Reframed Thought:** "My partner looked annoyed. I'm going to take a breath and assume he might be tired or thinking about something else, or I can gently ask him later if everything is okay without immediately assuming it's about me or a catastrophe."

The practice of identifying and challenging distorted thoughts takes consistent, compassionate effort. These unhelpful patterns are often deeply ingrained automatic shortcuts developed over a lifetime. With persistent practice, you will find yourself catching these thoughts earlier, questioning them more effectively, and ultimately choosing more balanced, realistic, and empowering interpretations of your experiences.

The direct intervention on your thought patterns is a cornerstone of emotional regulation, giving you profound control over your inner landscape and transforming it from a turbulent, reactive space to one of greater clarity and intentional response.

This is a crucial first step in your emotional mastery journey. When you learn to change your thoughts, you can begin to change your feelings, and ultimately, your actions. This internal work is the bedrock that will support the behavioral strategies for emotional regulation that you will explore in the following chapters, allowing you to not only navigate your emotional storms but also to build the resilience to weather them with greater strength and self-compassion.

CHAPTER 4:

BEHAVIORAL STRATEGIES FOR EMOTIONAL REGULATION

While challenging thoughts is crucial, it's only one part of the solution. When emotions run high, a woman's brain needs immediate, actionable steps to regain control. Dialectical Behavioral Therapy (DBT), a highly effective offshoot of CBT, provides a toolkit of such skills. DBT's four core skills are particularly well-suited for the challenges of ADHD in women: mindfulness, distress tolerance, emotion regulation, and interpersonal effectiveness.

Mindfulness helps a woman learn to observe her thoughts and emotions without judgment, grounding her in the present and reducing internal overwhelm. Distress tolerance is a "crisis survival" skill that teaches a woman how to cope with intense, painful emotions without resorting to unhelpful behaviors, a pattern sometimes observed in those with ADHD.

Emotion regulation teaches a woman how to manage and change intense, unwanted emotions. It involves understanding triggers and using proactive strategies to prevent emotional outbursts. Interpersonal effectiveness provides a woman with the tools to navigate relationships and communicate her needs effectively, reducing the emotional friction that can arise from misunderstandings and poor communication.

By learning and practicing these skills, a woman can gain greater control over her emotional reactions, transforming her emotional experience from an overwhelming rollercoaster into a more manageable journey.

The Role of Action in Emotional Mastery

A woman's brain needs immediate, actionable steps to regain control when emotions run high. While the cognitive work of identifying and challenging distorted thoughts is foundational, it's often not enough in the moment of an intense emotional surge. For the ADHD brain, which can have less effective inhibitory control from the prefrontal cortex, a profound emotional wave can sweep a woman away before her logical brain can fully engage. This is where behavioral strategies become a vital first line of defense.

The physical act of doing something, a movement, a sensory input, a grounding exercise, can create a crucial pause, a circuit-breaker that interrupts the emotional spiral and allows the nervous system to calm down.

DBT, which combines elements of cognitive behavioral therapy with mindfulness techniques, offers a comprehensive toolkit of these skills, empowering women to manage their impulsivity and emotional volatility. Rather than passively waiting for the overwhelming emotion to pass, these strategies encourage you to actively engage in behaviors that can calm your nervous system, strategically change your focus, or provide a healthy, constructive outlet for intense feelings, preventing them from spiraling out of control.

The skills are most effective when practiced regularly and integrated into your daily routine, as they become more readily available and effective when emotions become overwhelming.

The Foundational Skill: Mindfulness for Emotional Grounding

Mindfulness is a cornerstone of DBT and is often the first skill taught because it is a prerequisite for all the others. A practice of mindfulness helps you learn how to pay attention to the present moment without judgment, which is a powerful tool for a brain that is prone to racing thoughts, internal restlessness, and intense emotional surges.

A woman can use this tool to become more aware of her thoughts and emotions, which can decrease distress and improve her ability to respond effectively to difficult situations. The ability to simply observe a racing mind or an intense emotion without judgment is the first step toward managing it effectively. A moment of observation creates a crucial pause between stimulus and response, a space where a woman can recognize the emotion and choose a deliberate action rather than reacting impulsively.

This practice is a form of cognitive training that strengthens your brain's capacity for sustained attention and self-regulation over time, making you less likely to be derailed by a sudden emotional shift.

Riding the Wave: Distress Tolerance Skills

Distress tolerance skills are your "crisis survival" tools, designed for moments when emotions are so intense that you can't rationally process or change them. The goal is not to eliminate the distress but to endure it without resorting to impulsive, unhelpful, or harmful behaviors. For the ADHD brain, which often seeks immediate gratification or relief from discomfort, learning to "sit with" strong emotions is a powerful act of self-mastery.

- **The TIPP Skills:** TIPP is a powerful acronym that provides rapid physiological interventions to calm an activated nervous system. TIPP stands for:
    - **Temperature:** Splashing cold water on your face, or holding an ice pack on your wrists or neck, can activate the mammalian dive reflex, which naturally slows your heart rate and calms your nervous system.

- o **Intense Exercise:** Engaging in brief, intense physical activity, such as sprinting in place or a quick walk around the block, can help burn off excess emotional energy. A burst of physical movement is a direct and healthy way to discharge pent-up emotional energy that might otherwise lead to an emotional outburst.

- o **Paced Breathing:** Slowing your breathing down to a slower, more deliberate pace can directly impact your nervous system, shifting it from a "fight or flight" stress response to a more relaxed state. A simple exercise is to inhale slowly for four counts and exhale slowly for six counts, which can calm your body and mind.

- o **Paired Muscle Relaxation:** By tensing a muscle group very tightly for a few seconds and then completely relaxing it, you can create a tangible sense of relaxation that is felt throughout your body.

- **Radical Acceptance:** Some situations and intense emotions simply are. Fighting reality or trying to force a different emotional response only increases suffering. Radical acceptance is acknowledging the reality of a situation or an emotion without judgment, even if you don't like it or wish it were different. It's letting go of the struggle against what is. When faced with an unchangeable situation or an intense, unwanted emotion, you can internally (or even aloud) say, "I accept that I feel angry right now," or "This is a painful moment." The act of radical acceptance is not approval of the situation or emotion, but a release of the mental and emotional fight against reality, which can paradoxically reduce distress and free up energy for more constructive actions.

- **Wise Distraction:** Sometimes, when emotions are too intense to process rationally, a temporary, healthy distraction can be incredibly helpful to prevent escalation and give your nervous system time to cool down. A quick, absorbing task, like a puzzle or a short video game, can provide a healthy outlet that pulls your attention away from the intense emotion for a few minutes, allowing the intensity to subside to a more manageable level.

Managing the Ebb and Flow: Emotion Regulation Skills

Emotion regulation skills are about proactively managing emotions before they become overwhelming and reducing their intensity once they arise. This set of skills moves beyond simply tolerating distress to actively shaping your emotional experience.

- **Understanding Triggers:** A crucial step in emotion regulation is to become an expert on your own triggers. A woman can track her symptoms and their emotional impacts to understand the patterns that lead to intense feelings. For example, a woman with ADHD who also has PMDD might notice that her emotions become more difficult to manage in the days leading up to her period, which is a powerful trigger for emotional dysregulation. Identifying these patterns allows you to either avoid the trigger or proactively prepare for it with a plan of action.

- **Opposite Action:** A core DBT skill, opposite action is about identifying the unhelpful emotional urge and then doing the opposite of what that urge tells you to do. For example, if you are experiencing deep sadness and the urge is to withdraw from friends, the opposite action would be to reach out to a supportive friend. If you feel intense anxiety and the urge is to avoid a social situation, the opposite action would be to go to the event. Doing the opposite of an unhelpful emotional urge can directly change your emotional trajectory and prevent a negative spiral.

- **Building Positive Emotions:** Proactively building positive experiences into your life can make you more resilient to negative emotional swings. A woman can schedule activities that bring her joy, competence, or a sense of accomplishment. Research shows that engaging in creative activities such as painting, drawing, or writing can provide a positive outlet for expression and help channel overwhelming thoughts or emotions. Regular physical exercise also helps regulate mood and can serve as a powerful antidote to mental fatigue, helping you stay grounded. These small, consistent wins create a buffer of positive emotion that can help a woman weather the inevitable emotional storms with greater strength and stability.

Navigating Connections: Interpersonal Effectiveness Skills

Interpersonal effectiveness skills are a vital set of tools that help women with ADHD get their needs met, set boundaries, and maintain self-respect in relationships. A woman with ADHD often struggles with communication due to her tendency to interrupt, over-talk, or miss social cues, all of which can strain her relationships. These skills provide a structured way to navigate these challenges with greater clarity and effectiveness.

- **DEAR MAN:** The DEAR MAN acronym is a structured approach to assertive communication that is highly effective for women with ADHD who may struggle with being a people-pleaser to avoid rejection. The acronym stands for:
    - **Describe:** Describe the situation objectively, using facts, without judgment.
    - **Express:** Express your feelings using "I" statements.
    - **Assert:** Assert your needs or wishes clearly and respectfully.
    - **Reinforce:** Reinforce why they should help you by explaining the positive outcome.
    - **Mindful:** Stay mindful of your goals in the conversation.
    - **Appear Confident:** Appear confident and self-respecting.
    - **Negotiate:** Be willing to negotiate and offer a compromise.
- **"I" Statements:** Using "I" statements, which focus on your own feelings rather than the other person's actions, can de-escalate conflict and prevent the unhealthy "parent-child" dynamic that can develop in neurodiverse relationships. For example, instead of saying, "You never listen to me," a woman can say, "I feel unheard when I'm speaking and you're looking at your phone." By adopting these intentional communication

strategies, a woman can build a stronger, more empathetic connection with her loved ones.

A Holistic and Integrated Approach

By learning and practicing these behavioral skills, a woman can gain greater control over her emotional reactions, transforming her emotional experience from an overwhelming rollercoaster into a more manageable journey. The power of DBT lies in its integrated approach. It acknowledges that a woman's emotional world is a complex interplay of thoughts, feelings, and actions.

Learning how to identify and challenge unhelpful thoughts provides the cognitive map, while mastering these behavioral skills gives you the practical tools to navigate your inner landscape when the terrain becomes turbulent.

The journey to emotional mastery is not a destination but a continuous practice of learning and adaptation. There will be days when the strategies feel effortless and days when emotional surges feel overwhelming. The true strength lies not in achieving perfection, but in a woman's ability to consistently return to her toolkit, re-engage with her strategies, and approach each challenge with self-compassion. This is how you reclaim control over your emotional responses and build a foundation of genuine self-worth, emotional resilience, and ultimately, a more fulfilling life.

CHAPTER 5:

BUILDING EMOTIONAL RESILIENCE AND SELF-COMPASSION

Emotional resilience is a long-term goal that is built through a consistent practice of self-compassion. For women with ADHD who have internalized their struggles, a harsh inner critic is often a constant companion. That voice is a source of shame and a barrier to growth, often telling a woman that she is "not good enough" or that she will "fail anyway".

The antidote to this voice is to actively cultivate a supportive inner dialogue. A woman must consciously reframe her self-talk, replacing harsh judgments with understanding and encouragement. For instance, instead of saying, "I'm so useless for forgetting that," she can rephrase it as, "It's okay to forget things; my brain works differently. What can I do to help myself remember next time?"

Practicing compassionate self-talk is not about ignoring her challenges; it is about building a powerful inner ally who champions her efforts. By treating herself with the same kindness and empathy she would offer a close friend, a woman can begin to heal from a lifetime of self-blame and build a foundation of genuine self-worth. Inner kindness is a crucial catalyst for resilience, allowing her to learn from mistakes without being crippled by them and to navigate life's challenges with greater strength and self-acceptance.

The Science of Self-Criticism and Its Consequences

For many women with ADHD, the harsh inner critic is not a recent development but a voice that has been shaped by a lifetime of experiences. Undiagnosed ADHD can have profound impacts on self-esteem and feelings of self-worth. When referencing her childhood, one woman reported, "what I felt was I was actually a bad person... I was not an adequate human being."

The constant feeling that her struggles are personal flaws can lead to a pervasive sense of shame and self-blame, a pattern that research shows is significantly more common in women with ADHD than in men.

Neuroscience provides a clear explanation for why this internal dynamic is so damaging. Self-criticism and self-judgment trigger the brain's "threat-defense system." This automatic response releases stress hormones like cortisol and adrenaline, putting the body in a state of chronic stress and physiological arousal. Over time, this state of constant alert can lead to feelings of intense anxiety, fatigue, and even physical symptoms.

A continuous loop of self-blame and shame can deplete the emotional resources needed for resilience and self-regulation, making a woman more susceptible to burnout and emotional overwhelm. The pursuit of perfectionism is often a direct result of that intense self-criticism, as a woman tries to perform flawlessly to avoid any potential criticism from others or her inner voice.

The Three Pillars of Self-Compassion

Self-compassion, as defined by leading researcher Dr. Kristin Neff, is being warm and understanding toward yourself when you suffer, fail, or feel inadequate, rather than ignoring your pain or falling into self-criticism. It is not a sign of weakness or self-indulgence but a powerful physiological process that can fundamentally change the brain's structure and function. The practice is comprised of three core pillars that directly counteract the pain of the ADHD experience:

1. **Self-Kindness vs. Self-Judgment:** A woman with ADHD may habitually judge herself harshly for her symptoms, such as being late, forgetting an appointment, or struggling with a project. Self-kindness involves treating yourself gently instead of being critical and punitive. It means showing yourself patience and understanding, even when you stumble. Rather than falling into a spiral of self-criticism, a woman can respond to her own suffering with care and acceptance. This practice of self-kindness helps deactivate the brain's threat system and activates its care system, releasing feel-good hormones like oxytocin and endorphins.

2. **Common Humanity vs. Isolation:** When a woman with ADHD struggles with her symptoms, a common feeling is that she is alone in her suffering and that something is uniquely "wrong" with her. The struggle with organization, focus, and emotional regulation can feel like a private battle, leading to a deep sense of isolation. The principle of common humanity counters this by recognizing that all people experience difficulties and imperfections. A woman's struggles are part of the shared human experience. She is not alone in feeling this way. Recognizing that you are not unique in your difficulties helps to dismantle the shame and isolation that feeds the inner critic, fostering a sense of connection and belonging.

3. **Mindfulness vs. Over-identification:** The ADHD brain can struggle to find a middle ground between being completely disengaged from emotions and being entirely consumed by them. Over-identifying with an emotion means being so entangled in it that it feels all-consuming and unchangeable.

Mindfulness is the practice of having a non-judgmental awareness of your thoughts and emotions. It means observing negative emotions as they arise without judgment or falling into a spiral of rumination. A woman can notice an emotion, such as shame, without believing that she is her shame. This mindful stance creates a crucial distance from the emotional storm, allowing you to observe it rather than be swept away by it, and to choose a more thoughtful response.

The Neurobiological Antidote: Self-Compassion in Action

The biological foundations of self-compassion prove it is more than just a psychological construct. It represents a powerful physiological process that can fundamentally change the brain's structure and function, which results in improved emotional regulation and greater psychological well-being. The physiological effects go beyond the brain to impact the nervous system. Research shows that practicing self-compassion activates the parasympathetic nervous system, also known as the "rest and digest" response.

This activation leads to increased heart rate variability, which indicates better emotional regulation and stress resilience. By deactivating the brain's threat response, self-compassion enables the care system to release oxytocin and endorphins, which create feelings of safety and security.

Imaging studies reveal generating self-compassion uses similar neural processes as showing compassion for others, suggesting that being kind to ourselves activates the same caregiving circuits that help us support and nurture others. For women with ADHD who have often spent their lives trying to care for and please others to avoid criticism, turning that same well-practiced kindness inward is a powerful, restorative act.

Practical Tools for Cultivating an Inner Ally

The journey of building self-compassion is a continuous practice, not a quick fix. You can integrate these strategies into your daily life to slowly but surely reframe your inner dialogue and build a stronger foundation of resilience.

1. **Compassionate Rephrasing:** Actively challenge your inner critic by rephrasing harsh, judgmental thoughts into compassionate and realistic ones.

- **Harsh thought:** "I'm so lazy, I can't believe I procrastinated on that project again."
- **Self-compassionate rephrasing:** "That project was hard for my brain to get started on. Procrastination is a common ADHD struggle. What made this task particularly hard? What small step can I take now, or what strategy can I try next time?"
- **Harsh thought:** "I totally screwed up that conversation. I must have said something wrong, and now they hate me."
- **Self-compassionate rephrasing:** "I felt awkward in that conversation. It's okay to feel disappointed. My brain sometimes struggles with social cues, and that's not a personal failing. What's one thing I can learn for the next time, or can I ask them if I misinterpreted something?"

2. **Supportive Touch:** Your body can be a powerful tool for self-soothing and deactivating the threat response. When you feel overwhelmed or are being hard on yourself, use a comforting physical gesture.

- Place a hand on your heart and feel the warmth of your skin. Feel the rise and fall of your chest with each breath.
- Gently cup your own face in your hands, or give yourself a warm hug. The physical act of holding yourself with kindness provides a direct, physiological signal of safety to your nervous system.
- A woman can even imagine that they are the hands of someone who cares deeply for her.

3. **The Compassionate Anchor:** A woman with ADHD can use a simple, repetitive phrase to ground her in self-compassion when her inner critic becomes loud or she feels overwhelmed by a negative emotion. She can close her eyes, place her hands on her heart, and breathe deeply while repeating a compassionate mantra.

- "I'm here for you."
- "It's okay to make mistakes. My best is enough."
- "I'm doing my best and that's enough."
- "May I find peace, or happiness, or relief from my stress and suffering."

This is not a quick fix but a continuous practice that slowly rewires your brain's default emotional responses. It builds a powerful internal resource for emotional resilience, allowing you to navigate the ups and downs of life with greater inner stability and self-acceptance. By transforming your inner dialogue, you transform your entire emotional landscape, becoming your own most reliable guiding hand.

Conclusion: Your Emotional Strength

A powerful roadmap for navigating the inner emotional landscape of ADHD has been provided in this book. Your emotional intensity and reactivity have been validated as a neurobiological reality and you have been equipped with the tools to manage it. By learning to identify and challenge unhelpful thought patterns, implementing practical behavioral strategies from DBT, and cultivating a foundation of self-compassion, a woman can transform her relationship with her emotions.

She is no longer a passive victim of her feelings but an empowered guide who can navigate her inner world with intention and control. Emotional strength is the bedrock upon which all other areas of her life, from relationships to productivity, are built.

The Liberation of a Validated Experience

The journey through this book has been a process of profound self-discovery. For so long, the emotional struggles of a woman with ADHD may have felt like a chaotic internal battle, a torrent of feelings that were impossible to contain and often led to a deep sense of shame and inadequacy.

A prevailing narrative, often shaped by societal expectations and a lack of understanding, taught a woman that her emotional difficulties were a personal failing, a sign of being "overly sensitive" or "dramatic" rather than a legitimate aspect of her neurobiology. Research has consistently shown that women with ADHD tend to internalize their struggles and blame themselves, a pattern that fuels anxiety, depression, and a shattered sense of self-worth that is significantly more prevalent in women than in their male counterparts.

A crucial, liberating shift in perspective has been provided by this book, which illuminates the neurobiological realities behind these struggles. You now understand that your emotional intensity is a direct result of distinct brain function, particularly in a disconnect between the brain's emotional alarm system, the amygdala, and its "brakes" in the frontal cortex. You have learned that your emotions can feel "all-or-nothing" not because of a character flaw, but because your brain is less likely to inhibit big reactions.

This understanding is the bedrock of compassionate self-management. It allows a woman to move past a lifetime of self-recrimination and begin to approach her emotional challenges with curiosity and a strategic, problem-solving mindset, rather than with shame and frustration. Recognizing that your emotional reactivity is a neurobiological reality, not a personal failing, is the first and most powerful step toward reclaiming control over your inner world.

The Integrated System of Emotional Mastery

Learning how to master your emotional landscape is not about a single technique or a one-time fix. It is about building a cohesive, integrated system that works together to support your emotional well-being. The core of this system is built on a three-tiered approach that addresses your inner world from different angles: the cognitive, the behavioral, and the physiological.

1. The Cognitive Foundation: Challenging Unhelpful Thoughts You have learned that your thoughts are not facts; they are interpretations of reality that directly influence how you feel and act. The ADHD brain is particularly susceptible to "thinking traps" or cognitive distortions, such as "catastrophizing", jumping to the worst possible conclusion, or "mind reading," which involves assuming a negative judgment from others without evidence. That kind of negative self-talk often fuels intense emotional reactions, especially the debilitating pain of Rejection Sensitive Dysphoria (RSD).

By learning to pause and question these automatic thoughts, a woman can break the cycle of emotional reactivity. She has learned to become a "thought detective," meticulously examining the evidence for and against her thoughts and reframing her inner narrative from one of self-blame to one of understanding and compassion. This cognitive work creates a crucial pause, allowing the logical brain to engage before an emotional reaction takes over.

2. The Behavioral Toolkit: Active Regulation in the Moment When an emotional surge hits, a woman's brain needs immediate, actionable steps to regain control. The DBT toolkit you have explored provides concrete strategies to either calm your nervous system or strategically change your emotional state in the moment. You now have a repertoire of skills to use when emotions run high, such as the TIPP skills (Temperature, Intense Exercise, Paced Breathing, Paired Muscle Relaxation) that provide rapid physiological interventions to calm an activated nervous system. You have also learned about "Radical Acceptance," the powerful skill of letting go of the struggle against a painful reality, and "Opposite Action," which involves doing the opposite of what an unhelpful emotional urge tells you to do. These behavioral strategies are your first line of defense, empowering you to actively intervene in an emotional spiral rather than being a passive victim of your feelings.

3. The Physiological and Psychological Anchor: Self-Compassion and Resilience The work of emotional mastery is only sustainable when it is rooted in self-compassion. For women with ADHD, who have often internalized their struggles, a harsh inner critic is a constant companion. That voice is a source of shame and a barrier to growth, often telling a woman that she is "not good enough" or that she will "fail anyway". The antidote to this voice is to actively cultivate a supportive inner dialogue. You have learned that self-compassion, as defined by Dr. Kristin Neff, is a practice that activates the brain's "care system," releasing feel-good hormones like oxytocin and endorphins, and deactivating the threat-defense system that is triggered by self-criticism and shame. The consistent practice of self-kindness, recognizing your common humanity, and mindfulness provides a physiological and psychological buffer against emotional distress, allowing a woman to build a foundation of genuine self-worth. This inner kindness is a crucial catalyst for resilience, allowing you to learn from mistakes without being crippled by them and to navigate life's challenges with greater strength and self-acceptance.

The Bedrock for a Balanced Life

Emotional strength is not a skill that operates in isolation. It is the bedrock upon which all other areas of a woman's life are built. Without emotional mastery, even the most robust organizational systems or the most diligent time management strategies can crumble under the weight of an overwhelming emotional surge or a period of intense mental fatigue.

- **A Bridge to Sharpened Focus (Book 2):** Emotional chaos fragments attention. A brain that is constantly in a state of emotional turmoil is a brain that has less mental bandwidth for sustained focus and deep work. The constant, conscious effort to manage internalized emotional symptoms depletes mental energy reserves, creating what is known as the "ADHD tax" that leaves a woman mentally exhausted and more susceptible to burnout. Emotional mastery provides a sense of calm and clarity that allows the internal chaos to subside, freeing up immense cognitive bandwidth that can be redirected toward purposeful focus.

- **A Catalyst for Nurturing Relationships (Book 5):** Emotional intensity and reactivity, especially RSD, are major sources of friction in relationships. By learning to identify and challenge unhelpful thought patterns and practicing the "STOP" skill before reacting, a woman is better equipped to navigate conflict with greater intentionality. She can use "I" statements to communicate her needs effectively without blaming her partner, which can de-escalate conflict and prevent the unhealthy "parent-child" dynamic that can sometimes develop in neurodiverse relationships. A more stable emotional baseline, achieved through the practice of these skills, provides a more predictable and reliable emotional base for building and sustaining meaningful relationships.

- **A Foundation for Productivity (Book 3):** Emotional dysregulation, low frustration tolerance, and the fear of failure can lead to task paralysis and procrastination. The intense shame and self-criticism that often accompany a woman's struggles with productivity can be so debilitating that she avoids tasks altogether rather than risking imperfection or criticism. Emotional resilience and self-compassion provide the mental fortitude to push through difficult projects and recover from setbacks. By developing a supportive inner ally, a woman is better able to learn from her mistakes, accept that progress is more important than perfection, and continue to engage with her goals, even when the initial novelty wears off. Emotional strength is the fuel for consistent action, transforming a cycle of avoidance into a journey of accomplishment.

A woman is no longer merely coping with her emotional world; she is actively shaping it with intention and control. The journey to emotional mastery is not a destination but a continuous practice of learning and adaptation. There will be days when the strategies feel effortless and days when emotional surges feel overwhelming. The true strength lies not in achieving perfection but in a woman's ability to consistently return to her toolkit, re-engage with her strategies, and approach each challenge with self-compassion.

You now have the blueprint to navigate a challenging emotional landscape with greater inner stability, resilience, and strength, giving you a powerful foundation for building the extraordinary life you are capable of living.

Reflection Questions

- The book highlights how emotional dysregulation is a hallmark of the female ADHD experience. Can you identify a common trigger for an intense emotional reaction you experience? What CBT tool (e.g., challenging a thought) or DBT skill (e.g., Opposite Action) can you use the next time you feel this way?
- How has the practice of self-compassion changed your inner dialogue? What is one specific, kind thing you can tell yourself the next time you make a mistake or feel like a "failure?"The

text talks about emotional strength as a foundation for other areas of life. How does managing your emotions affect your ability to stay organized or focused?

BOOK FIVE:

MANAGE YOUR MONEY & RELATIONSHIPS: ESSENTIAL SKILLS FOR THE ADHD WOMAN

INTRODUCTION:

THE ADULTING CHALLENGE

For many women with ADHD, the transition into adulthood brings a unique set of challenges related to money and relationships. These are two vital areas of life that require sophisticated executive functions, such as planning, organization, impulse control, and emotional regulation, which are often compromised by ADHD symptoms.

The result is a persistent feeling of being overwhelmed and a consistent struggle to manage finances and nurture relationships in a way that feels seamless to a neurotypical individual. The consequences of these struggles are not just financial or social; they create a pervasive feeling of inadequacy and amplify the shame that so many women with ADHD already feel. This book will provide an honest, evidence-based guide to navigating these challenges, empowering women to build systems that support their financial and social well-being.

The journey into adulthood is a period defined by an increasing need for independence and self-management, a reality that can be particularly daunting for a woman with ADHD. Executive functions, the brain's "command center" for planning, organizing, and controlling impulses, are crucial for navigating this transition successfully.

Difficulties with these core mental processes directly impact a woman's ability to manage her finances, build and maintain a career, and nurture healthy, stable relationships, all of which are benchmarks of a successful adult life. For many women, these struggles are invisible, a constant, private battle fought against a neurobiological reality that makes "adulting" feel like an impossible task. The gap between the societal expectation of a put-together, organized, and emotionally mature woman and her internal experience of chaos and overwhelm can lead to a profound and debilitating sense of shame and self-blame.

The Financial Toll: The "ADHD Tax" on Your Wallet and Well-Being

The financial challenges faced by women with ADHD are a direct result of core ADHD symptoms and are not a reflection of their intelligence or character. Research provides a clear picture of what can be called the "financial ADHD tax," a measurable cost that living with ADHD can impose over a lifetime.

A 2020 study found that between the ages of 25 and 30, adults with ADHD show considerably slower growth in income and savings and often remain financially dependent on their families. By age 30, they earn 37% less per month than their peers, and the projected retirement gap is staggering: 40% less net worth in the best-case scenario, potentially ballooning to 64% less, about $431,000, when accounting for inconsistent saving patterns.

These sobering statistics are a direct consequence of ADHD-related executive function challenges, particularly impulsivity, time blindness, and poor organization.

- **The Impulsivity of Spending:** A primary cause of financial instability is impulsivity, which can lead to spontaneous purchases that undermine budgeting and saving goals. The ADHD brain's love of novelty and search for stimulation often makes it susceptible to the allure of new hobbies or expensive gadgets, which can lead to significant financial and physical clutter. These are often not deliberate or malicious acts but a genuine difficulty in delaying gratification or considering the long-term consequences of a financial decision in the face of an immediate reward. A key strategy to combat this is creating a crucial pause before a purchase, perhaps by physically writing down an item before buying it.

- **The Cost of Time Blindness:** A significant factor contributing to financial distress is time blindness, a difficulty in accurately perceiving the passage of time that leads to rushed decisions, late payments, and the accumulation of late fees and fines. A woman may genuinely believe she has "plenty of time" to pay a bill, only to find the deadline has passed, leading to a financial penalty that could have easily been avoided. This isn't intentional negligence but a neurocognitive reality that makes it challenging to plan and prioritize based on future deadlines, as the future can often feel less "real" than the present.

- **Disorganization and Avoidance:** Poor planning and a struggle to stay organized make it difficult to manage paperwork, keep track of bills, and stick to a budget, which further contributes to financial instability. A woman might feel so overwhelmed by the thought of sitting down with a budget or sorting through a pile of bills that she avoids the task entirely, a pattern of spontaneous and avoidant decision-making that is common in individuals with ADHD. The avoidance of these tasks is not laziness but a coping mechanism for the immense cognitive load and feelings of overwhelm they can trigger.

The Relational Toll: The Intricacies of Neurodiverse Dynamics

Relationships, while a source of great joy, can also be a mirror for a woman's underlying ADHD symptoms. Communication, in particular, can be a major source of friction. One of the most common challenges is difficulty with active listening, where a woman's mind may wander or "zone out" during a conversation, leading her partner to feel unheard or unprioritized.

This is often compounded by impulsive interruptions, where a woman might blurt out her thoughts or finish a sentence because she fears she will forget what she wanted to say. A woman's communication style can be misinterpreted as disinterest, when in reality, she is battling a fragmented attention span.

The challenges of ADHD in relationships are further complicated by the inherent gender differences in symptom presentation and societal expectations. While men may exhibit externalized, hyperactive symptoms, women's inattentive symptoms are often internalized, leading to a greater tendency to self-blame and a shattered sense of self-worth.

These internalization tendencies are a direct conflict with societal expectations for women to be nurturing, emotionally available, and cooperative, particularly within their families and relationships.

A common dynamic that can emerge in neurodiverse couples is a "parent-child" relationship, where in an attempt to help the ADHD partner better organize their lives or remember tasks, the neurotypical partner may unwittingly leave the ADHD partner feeling like a scolded child. This can lead to avoidance or dishonesty from the ADHD partner and can trigger a symptom known as Rejection Sensitive Dysphoria (RSD), an extreme emotional responsiveness to perceived rejection or criticism.

For a woman with ADHD, a partner who calmly expresses a concern may be perceived through the "lens of ADHD" as being overly critical or micromanaging, which can lead to an intense emotional reaction and a breakdown in communication.

The challenges of living with ADHD in women extend beyond romantic relationships to friendships and social dynamics as well. Research indicates that women with ADHD have a harder time forming and maintaining friendships, which can lead to painful feelings of loneliness and a sense of never "fitting in".

This is often a consequence of being socially rejected in childhood and a struggle to meet the social expectations of others, such as suppressing the urge to interrupt or showing up on time. A lack of a well-developed social support network for women with ADHD is particularly damaging, as a strong social network can serve as a vital buffer against stress and emotional turmoil, a coping mechanism that women are more likely to rely on than men.

Shame and Inadequacy: The Amplifying Emotional Burden

The consequences of these financial and relational struggles are not just external; they create a pervasive and amplifying emotional burden. A lifetime of feeling misunderstood, coupled with a string of failures rooted in ADHD symptoms, can lead to a deep-seated belief that a woman is inadequate or "not good enough." The constant pressure to meet impossible standards and the perpetual cycle of feeling overwhelmed and behind can erode a woman's self-esteem and feed a pervasive sense of shame.

Without a diagnosis or a framework to understand her struggles, a woman may attribute her difficulties with organization, focus, and emotional regulation to personal flaws, a pattern that fuels anxiety, depression, and a shattering sense of self-worth. A woman with undiagnosed ADHD reported feeling "what I felt was I was actually a bad person... I was not an adequate human being."

These painful feelings are often made worse by the societal expectation for women to "do it all", to excel in a career, maintain an organized home, and be an emotionally available partner and mother, a "double burden" that directly conflicts with the core symptoms of ADHD. When a woman with ADHD inevitably falls short of these unrealistic standards, the shame can be immense and debilitating, leading to a self-loathing that can be a source of significant distress.

This book is a direct response to this reality. It acknowledges that a woman's struggles with money and relationships are not a sign of a character flaw but a neurobiological reality that requires a new set of tools. By providing an honest, evidence-based guide to navigating these challenges, it aims to empower women to build systems that support their financial and social well-being. A woman can move from a place of chronic overwhelm to a place of integrated success by confronting financial challenges with systems that work for her ADHD brain, strengthening her communication with loved ones, and actively building a community that validates her experience. She can then build a truly resilient and fulfilling life.

CHAPTER **1**:

MONEY AND THE ADHD BRAIN

The financial challenges faced by women with ADHD are a direct result of core ADHD symptoms and are not a reflection of their intelligence or character. Research provides a clear picture of what can be called the "financial ADHD tax," a measurable cost that living with ADHD can impose over a lifetime.

Studies have found that people with ADHD have lower savings, higher debt, and slower income growth than their peers. This is a direct consequence of ADHD-related executive function challenges.

A primary cause of this is impulsivity, which can lead to spontaneous purchases that undermine budgeting and saving goals. The ADHD brain's love of novelty and search for stimulation often makes it susceptible to the allure of new hobbies or expensive gadgets, which can lead to significant financial and physical clutter.

Another significant factor is time blindness, a difficulty in accurately perceiving the passage of time that leads to rushed decisions, late payments, and the accumulation of late fees and fines. Poor planning and organization make it difficult to manage paperwork, keep track of bills, and stick to a budget, which further contributes to financial instability.

The "Financial ADHD Tax": A Lifelong Cost

The financial struggles of women with ADHD are not merely isolated incidents of poor judgment; they are a pervasive and measurable phenomenon with long-term consequences. A 2020 study, which followed individuals from childhood into adulthood, painted a sobering picture of the "financial ADHD tax".

The research found that between the ages of 25 and 30, adults with ADHD show considerably slower growth in income and savings, and often remain financially dependent on their families. A projected retirement gap is staggering: a person with ADHD could have 40% less net worth in the best-case scenario, potentially ballooning to 64% less when accounting for inconsistent saving patterns, which is a hallmark of the condition.

These patterns persist regardless of education level or income, highlighting that the challenges are not rooted in a lack of knowledge but in the neurobiological difficulties that make traditional financial management so difficult.

The research is clear that even individuals who had only moderate ADHD symptoms in childhood, and may have never received a diagnosis, fared worse financially as adults compared to their peers without the condition. This suggests that the more severe the ADHD symptoms, the stronger the effect on financial distress.

A woman may not be aware that her financial difficulties are a symptom of her ADHD, leading her to internalize her struggles and blame herself, a pattern that can lead to feelings of confusion, anxiety, and depression that further demotivate her from making positive changes.

Impulsivity: The Dopamine-Driven Spending

The ADHD brain's natural inclination toward novelty and immediate gratification is a primary driver of financial instability. The dysregulated dopamine system, which is involved in motivation and reward, makes it difficult to delay gratification for a more distant reward, such as saving for retirement. A spontaneous purchase of a new gadget or a new hobby provides an immediate hit of stimulation and dopamine, which feels far more compelling to the ADHD brain than the abstract, long-term reward of financial security.

This impulsivity can lead to a cycle of overspending, acquiring significant debt, and investing valuable time and money into a hobby of the day, only to lose interest and move on to the next.

The modern retail environment is uniquely designed to trigger this impulsivity. Retail apps and online platforms often "gamify" shopping with points, streaks, flash sales, and "limited time" offers that can trigger impulsivity. To combat this, a woman can create a crucial "pause" between an impulse and a purchase.

Even if a perfect record isn't kept, the simple act of writing down a purchase before making it can be a powerful tool for preventing impulsive buys. This provides a moment for executive functions to intervene and reconsider the long-term impact of a purchase before it's made. Additionally, setting up a separate account for "spontaneous" or lifestyle purchases can create a boundary that prevents impulsive spending from derailing a budget.

Time Blindness: The Cost of Chronic Lateness

A significant and often misunderstood contributor to financial challenges is time blindness, a difficulty in accurately perceiving the passage of time that leads to rushed decisions, late payments, and the accumulation of late fees and fines. A woman with ADHD may genuinely believe she has "plenty of time" to pay a bill, only to find the deadline has passed, leading to a financial penalty that could have easily been avoided.

The future can often feel less "real" than the present, making it challenging to prioritize tasks based on their true time sensitivity. This isn't intentional negligence but a neurocognitive reality that requires external support systems to manage effectively.

The financial costs of time blindness can add up over a lifetime, from late fees on bills to a lack of emergency savings due to an inability to prioritize long-term benefits over short-term rewards. To counteract this, automation is a powerful strategy.

Setting up automatic bill payments, investment transfers, and savings contributions to happen immediately after payday eliminates the need for constant decision-making and manual follow-through. This system bypasses the cognitive challenges of time blindness and provides a reliable safety net for a woman's finances. Using multiple reminders or scheduling a specific day each month to pay bills can also serve as an external cue to manage these tasks proactively.

The Cognitive Hurdles of Planning and Organization

Traditional financial management advice often relies on the very executive functions that are compromised by ADHD: sustained focus, planning, and organization. For many women with ADHD, the symptoms make it harder to track expenses, remember due dates, stay organized with bills and documents, and focus on financial statements and budgets. The very act of trying to focus on setting a monthly budget or calculating expenses can feel overwhelming and is often put off or avoided entirely, a pattern of avoidant and spontaneous decision-making that is common in individuals with ADHD.

To overcome these hurdles, a woman can leverage a new set of tools and strategies:

- **Visual Systems:** Many people with ADHD are visual thinkers. Using budgeting apps with charts and graphs, creating simple visual budget boards, or using color-coded systems can be particularly helpful. These visual aids make abstract numbers more tangible and easier for the ADHD brain to process, reducing the feeling of being overwhelmed.

- **Technology to the Rescue:** Utilizing expense and money-tracking apps can help a woman stay on top of her spending in real time, rather than trying to revisit purchases later. Setting up automatic payments and transfers ensures that financial tasks are completed reliably without the need for manual initiation.

- **External Support:** For tasks that require sustained focus, such as setting up a budget, the strategy of "body doubling" can be highly effective. A woman can work alongside a friend, either in person or virtually, to provide a subtle sense of accountability and structure that makes it easier to start and remain on task.

By confronting these financial challenges with systems that work for the ADHD brain, a woman can move from a place of chronic overwhelm to a place of integrated success. This is not about becoming a financial expert overnight but about building a supportive framework that mitigates the inherent challenges of ADHD. It's about understanding that financial well-being doesn't evolve from budgets, math, and spreadsheets alone; it evolves from a healthy financial mindset and a toolbox of strategies that empower you to take control of your financial life.

Table: Common Financial Pitfalls and Evidence-Based Solutions

Common Financial Pitfall	ADHD Symptom Connection	Evidence-Based Solution
Impulse spending	Impulsivity, novelty-seeking	Automate savings and bill payments; create a "pause" by physically writing down purchases.
Late bill payments	Time blindness, disorganization	Use automatic bill payments and set multiple reminders; schedule a specific day to pay bills.
Poor budgeting	Executive dysfunction, difficulty with sustained focus	Use visual budgeting apps with charts and graphs; use body doubling to get the task done.

Common Financial Pitfall	ADHD Symptom Connection	Evidence-Based Solution
Inconsistent saving	Preference for short-term rewards	Automate transfers to a separate savings account immediately after payday to make it a non-negotiable habit.

CHAPTER 2:

COMMUNICATION IN RELATIONSHIPS

Relationships, while a source of great joy, can also be a mirror for a woman's underlying ADHD symptoms. Communication, in particular, can be a major source of friction. One of the most common challenges is difficulty with active listening, where a woman's mind may wander or "zone out" during a conversation, leading her partner to feel unheard or unprioritized.

Often, a woman might blurt out her thoughts or finish a sentence because she fears she will forget what she wanted to say, which further compounds this. To combat a fragmented attention span, practicing mindfulness and active listening is crucial. Consciously putting away distractions and paraphrasing what the other person is saying helps to ensure comprehension.

To navigate difficult conversations, a shift from blaming to understanding is essential. Using "I" statements, which focus on one's own feelings rather than the other person's actions, can de-escalate conflict and prevent the unhealthy "parent-child" dynamic that can develop in neurodiverse relationships.

For example, instead of saying, "You never listen to me," a woman can say, "I feel unheard when I'm speaking and you're looking at your phone." By adopting intentional communication strategies, a woman can build a stronger, more empathetic connection with her loved ones.

The Neurobiology of Relational Friction

The communication challenges that arise in relationships affected by ADHD are not a reflection of a woman's desire to be a good partner; they are a direct consequence of a brain that is wired differently. The ADHD brain often has a harder time concentrating than a neurotypical brain and a reduced ability to filter out irrelevant stimuli.

A woman's mind can either "hypofocus" (a daydream-like state) or "hyperfocus" (a state of intense focus on a single subject, and only that subject), both of which can create a powerful external appearance of not paying attention during conversations.

Her partner may believe she is not interested in what they have to say, which can lead to resentment over time, even though she is genuinely trying to listen.

A woman's tendency to impulsively interrupt or blurt out her thoughts is also rooted in this neurobiology. The brain's working memory can feel like a sieve, making it difficult to hold a thought for even a few moments. A woman may feel an intense urge to speak immediately, fearing that the thought will be lost forever if she waits for her turn in the conversation. While a neurotypical individual may interpret this as a lack of social graces, it is, in fact, a symptom of a neurocognitive reality.

A constant barrage of internal thoughts can also make it difficult for a woman with ADHD to pick up on social cues, read body language, or be attuned to the emotions of others, which can be a significant source of friction in social dynamics and lead to a painful sense of "never fitting in."

The Parent-Child Dynamic and the Pain of RSD

A particularly difficult dynamic can emerge in relationships where one partner has ADHD, often resembling a parent-child relationship. In an attempt to help their partner better organize their lives or remember tasks, a neurotypical partner may unintentionally take on the role of a taskmaster or a reminder, leaving the ADHD partner feeling like a scolded child.

This can lead to avoidance, dishonesty, or even resentment from the ADHD partner and can trigger a significant symptom of ADHD known as "rejection sensitivity."

Rejection Sensitive Dysphoria (RSD), while not a formal diagnosis in diagnostic manuals, is a term used to describe an "extreme emotional responsiveness and anxiety in anticipation of, or in response to, perceived rejection or criticism from others."

For a woman with ADHD, who may have spent a lifetime internalizing her struggles, a partner who calmly expresses a concern may be perceived through the "lens of ADHD" as being overly critical or micromanaging. This can trigger an immediate, overwhelming emotional pain that can feel physically agonizing and lead to a disproportionate emotional reaction that compromises the relationship and the well-being of both partners.

The behaviors and coping mechanisms that stem from this profound sensitivity can ironically lead to more rejection, creating a challenging and painful cycle in the relationship. To break free from this cycle, both partners must understand that RSD is a real and often debilitating experience for the ADHD partner and not a deliberate choice to be "difficult."

Building a Bridge: Strategies for Effective Communication

Communication is the bedrock of any healthy relationship. For couples navigating ADHD, being intentional and strategic about how they communicate can build a powerful bridge of empathy and understanding.

- **Practice Active and Mindful Listening:** Active listening is paramount to fostering trust and deepening understanding. To combat a fragmented attention span, a woman can consciously turn off distractions, such as putting down her phone and closing her laptop. Making eye contact and turning her body towards her partner shows she is fully engaged. Another powerful technique is to paraphrase or use reflective responses. After her partner speaks, she can say, "So, what you're saying is..." to confirm her understanding. This not only shows she is actively listening but also helps to clarify any misunderstandings before they can escalate into conflict. A woman can also ask open-ended questions to encourage her partner to share more about their thoughts and feelings, which shows genuine interest and creates space for deeper conversations.

- **Use "I" Statements to Express Needs:** When discussing difficult topics or expressing emotions, using "I" statements is essential to de-escalate conflict and prevent the other person from feeling blamed. Rather than saying, "You never help me with the chores," a woman can say, "I feel overwhelmed when I'm the only one taking care of the laundry." This approach shifts the focus from the other person's actions to your own feelings, which can prevent defensiveness and open the door for a more productive conversation.

- **Structured Conversations and "Relationship Roundtables":** Spontaneous, emotionally charged conversations are often difficult for the ADHD brain to navigate. A woman's emotional intensity can lead to impulsive reactions and regrettable words that she later regrets, which is why a more structured approach to important discussions is so effective. Setting aside a specific time each week for a "Relationship Roundtable" can be one of the single most useful strategies for improving communication and connection. This is a designated, distraction-free time to discuss logistics, plan for the week, and address any ongoing challenges. By tackling these issues in a structured, calm environment, both partners can feel heard and avoid the emotional friction that can arise from having a difficult conversation in the heat of the moment.

- **Create a Shared Language and External Systems:** A powerful tool for managing emotionally charged conversations is to create a shared language or signal that both partners can use. A pre-agreed "safe word" or signal can be used when a conversation is becoming too overwhelming for one partner, providing a non-confrontational way to pause or exit a difficult situation without it feeling like a rejection. Furthermore, a woman can leverage external systems to offload the mental burden of remembering things. Using shared digital calendars, chore charts on a whiteboard, or reminder apps can shift the responsibility of remembering tasks off the non-ADHD partner, which can reduce resentment and prevent the parent-child dynamic from taking hold.

- **Education, Empathy, and a Shared Journey:** A foundational strategy is for both partners to educate themselves about ADHD. Understanding how ADHD works in the brain and how it uniquely impacts a woman's presentation of symptoms can help reduce blame and increase understanding. A woman can gently educate her partner about the neurobiological reasons for her struggles, helping them understand that her behaviors are not a reflection of a lack of care but a result of a different brain wiring. In a relationship with ADHD, both partners are equally responsible for the success of the relationship. Open communication and a shared commitment to building new structures and methods of communication that work for both partners are crucial.

Nurturing relationships and improving communication for women with ADHD is an ongoing process of self-awareness, intentional action, and open dialogue. By applying these strategies, a woman can build a more resilient, empathetic, and fulfilling connection with her loved ones, transforming her relationships from a source of frustration and misunderstanding into a wellspring of support and joy.

CHAPTER 3:

NAVIGATING SHARED RESPONSIBILITIES AND SOCIAL DYNAMICS

Beyond communication, shared responsibilities and social interactions present a unique set of challenges for women with ADHD. A neurotypical partner can become frustrated by a woman's disorganization or her difficulty with task initiation on household chores.

The partner may feel that they are taking care of everything on their own, a situation that often leads to resentment. This is a direct result of the woman's struggle with executive function and is not a lack of caring.

One powerful solution is to externalize shared responsibilities with visual aids, such as a whiteboard chore chart, and to proactively break down larger tasks into smaller, manageable steps with scheduled reminders.

In broader social dynamics, women with ADHD often face significant barriers. Research indicates that they have a harder time forming and maintaining friendships, which can lead to feelings of loneliness and a sense of never "fitting in".

This is often a consequence of being socially rejected in childhood and a struggle to meet the social expectations of others, such as suppressing the urge to interrupt or showing up on time. It is important to acknowledge this struggle and actively seek out communities that are affirming and supportive, where a woman can feel seen and accepted for who she is.

The Mental Load of Shared Responsibilities

The challenges of managing shared responsibilities for a woman with ADHD go far beyond the physical act of doing a chore. Research from Gallup News shows that married or partnered women in the U.S. still shoulder the primary responsibility for the majority of household chores, including laundry, cleaning, and preparing meals.

Even in households where both partners work, women still perform the bulk of the domestic work and childcare planning. The expectation for women to "do it all", to excel in a career while also flawlessly managing the home, creates a "double burden" that directly conflicts with the core symptoms of ADHD. This immense, often invisible, mental burden is a significant drain on executive function, a set of cognitive skills that are essential for planning, prioritizing, and completing tasks.

For a woman with ADHD, a disorganized or neglected household is not a sign of laziness but a reflection of her brain's executive function challenges. She may struggle with task initiation, a "just can't start" syndrome where the thought of organizing a room or doing a pile of laundry feels so overwhelming that she is paralyzed.

Poor planning and organization make it difficult to keep track of a household schedule or to consistently follow through on chores, leading to a home environment that feels chaotic and unpredictable. When a neurotypical partner is forced to constantly remind their partner with ADHD about tasks, a difficult and unhealthy "parent-child" dynamic can emerge in the relationship. The neurotypical partner may unknowingly take on the role of a taskmaster, while the ADHD partner may feel like a scolded child, which can lead to resentment, avoidance, and a profound sense of shame for not being able to manage daily life like a competent adult.

Research shows that neurodiverse couples can develop this dynamic when one partner consistently feels underappreciated for the extra effort they take to manage the household and the other partner feels criticized and misunderstood for their struggles. This dynamic undermines the core sense of partnership and respect that is vital to a healthy relationship.

The Impact on Social Dynamics

The same executive function and emotional regulation challenges that affect a woman's home life also create significant barriers in her broader social dynamics and friendships. Research indicates that women with ADHD have a harder time forming and maintaining friendships, which can lead to painful feelings of loneliness and a profound sense of never "fitting in".

A study in girls with ADHD found that those who were hyperactive or impulsive were "socially rejected" by peers, while those with the quieter, inattentive subtype were "socially neglected," or simply left out of social groups. These patterns persist into adulthood, a reality that is particularly painful for women who have a greater need for social acceptance and connection than men.

A woman's struggles to meet neurotypical social expectations are often rooted in her ADHD symptoms. She may have difficulty with active listening, where her mind wanders or "zones out" during conversations, leading her partner or friends to feel unheard or unprioritized. A woman with ADHD may also struggle to suppress the urge to interrupt in conversation because she fears she will forget what she wanted to say. The inability to consistently meet these social expectations, such as showing up on time for social commitments or curbing the tendency to talk too much, can lead to social rejection or the perception of being rude, which can take a significant toll on a woman's self-esteem and feed her belief that she is unworthy of authentic connection.

This is further compounded by a woman's tendency to struggle with reading social cues or body language, a challenge that can make navigating complex social situations difficult and anxiety-inducing.

The Social Cost of Masking

The constant effort to mask ADHD symptoms carries a profound social cost for women. Masking is a coping mechanism where a woman develops sophisticated behaviors to hide her struggles and appear "neurotypical" to the outside world. For example, a woman might meticulously maintain a façade of punctuality by building in extra time for everything, a strategy she developed to combat her innate time blindness and avoid the social consequences of being late. Another might learn to pretend to take notes in a meeting to hide the fact that she is "zoning out" or has a "thousand-yard stare".

While masking may be a survival strategy developed to avoid social rejection, it can also lead to chronic loneliness and a debilitating sense of not being able to be one's authentic self. A woman may feel like an impostor, constantly fearing that her true self will be discovered and she will be rejected. This painful experience is particularly damaging and reinforces the low self-esteem and shame that are so prevalent in women with ADHD.

The stress of this constant, exhausting effort to appear "non-ADHD" is an invisible burden that can lead to a lifetime of internalized shame, anxiety, and depression, and can also prevent a woman from forming the robust social support network that is so vital for her well-being.

Building a Bridge: Strategies for Shared Responsibilities

Overcoming the challenges of shared responsibilities requires a shift from blame and frustration to a collaborative, solution-oriented mindset. The goal is to build external systems that compensate for internal inconsistencies and to work as a team to create a household that is supportive for everyone.

- **Externalize Shared Responsibilities:** Do not rely on one person's internal memory or emotional bandwidth to manage the household. Use visual aids, such as a whiteboard chore chart, a shared digital calendar, or a simple analog system to track all household responsibilities. This external system offloads the mental burden from the neurotypical partner, reduces the need for reminders, and provides a clear, objective record of what needs to be done.

- **Divide Tasks by Strengths, Not Fairness:** Rather than trying to divide all tasks equally, divide them in a way that leverages each partner's unique strengths. If one person thrives on spontaneity and the other on structure, split responsibilities accordingly. Perhaps one person handles tasks that are more fluid or require a quick burst of energy, while the other manages more routine or administrative tasks like paying bills.

- **Break Down Overwhelming Tasks:** Large household tasks can trigger "ADHD paralysis" or overwhelm. Break down larger tasks into smaller, more manageable steps with scheduled reminders. For instance, instead of "Clean the entire kitchen," a more manageable step would be "Load and start the dishwasher," or "Wipe down the countertops." A successful completion of a small task provides a small but satisfying burst of dopamine that builds momentum for the next step.

- **Have a Weekly "Relationship Roundtable":** Set aside a specific, non-distracting time each week to sit down with your partner and discuss logistics, shared responsibilities, and upcoming plans. Calling it a "Relationship Roundtable" can make the conversation feel less like a confrontational "chore meeting" and more like a collaborative team huddle. This dedicated time allows for a calm, structured discussion of issues before they can escalate into a reactive argument in the heat of the moment.

Building a Network: Strategies for Social Dynamics

Navigating social dynamics and building meaningful friendships for a woman with ADHD requires a proactive and compassionate approach that acknowledges her unique challenges while also seeking out supportive connections.

- **Gently Educate Your Loved Ones:** An important strategy is to gently educate your loved ones about ADHD, helping them to understand that your behaviors are not a reflection of a lack of care but a result of a different brain wiring. You can explain that your tendency to interrupt is because you fear you will forget your thought if you wait, or that your struggle with time is due to a neurocognitive difference called "time blindness". This fosters empathy and can help reduce the blame and misunderstanding that so often arise from these situations.

- **Seek Out Affirming Communities:** Actively seek out communities that are validating and affirming, where a woman can feel seen and accepted for who she is. This can be through online forums, support groups, or other channels where she can connect with others who share her experience. This practice of finding her community is an essential step towards healing from a lifetime of masking and building a foundation of genuine self-acceptance and belonging.

- **Create a Shared Language for Overwhelm:** For a woman who struggles with emotional and sensory overload in social situations, having a pre-agreed "safe word" or signal with a partner or close friend can be a non-confrontational way to pause or exit a challenging situation without it feeling like a rejection. For example, a woman could signal that she needs a few minutes to reset, and her partner would know to step outside with her for a moment or give her space to breathe without it feeling like an insult or a rejection.

- **Embrace Self-Compassion:** Acknowledging the social challenges of ADHD is not about excusing your behavior, but about building a foundation of self-compassion that allows you to approach your struggles with curiosity and kindness rather than shame and self-blame. Women with ADHD are more likely to internalize their struggles, leading to a deep sense of shame and feelings of worthlessness. By reframing her struggles as a neurobiological reality and celebrating her genuine efforts to connect, a woman can begin to heal from a lifetime of hurt and build the confidence to form authentic, lasting bonds.

Nurturing relationships and navigating social dynamics for women with ADHD is an ongoing process of self-awareness, intentional action, and open dialogue. By applying these strategies, a woman will not only reduce friction and misunderstanding but also build deeper, more resilient connections that enrich her life and provide invaluable support on her journey to a balanced existence.

CHAPTER 4:

THE SOCIAL COST: MASKING, REJECTION, AND FINDING YOUR COMMUNITY

The constant effort to mask ADHD symptoms carries a profound social cost for women. While masking may be a survival strategy developed to avoid social rejection, it can also lead to chronic loneliness and a debilitating sense of not being able to be one's authentic self.

A woman may feel like an impostor, constantly fearing that her true self will be discovered and she will be rejected. An experience like this is particularly painful and reinforces the low self-esteem and shame that are so prevalent in women with ADHD. The struggle is further compounded by the fact that women with ADHD are often less successful at forming a robust social support network, which can serve as a vital buffer against stress and emotional turmoil.

To break free from this cycle, a woman must begin to cultivate a more compassionate and accepting relationship with her neurodiversity. She can start by gently educating her loved ones about her ADHD, helping them understand that her behaviors are not a reflection of a lack of care but a result of a different brain wiring. She must also actively seek out and find communities that are validating and affirming. Finding her community is an essential step towards healing from a lifetime of masking and building a foundation of genuine self-acceptance.

The Silent Burden of Masking

For women with ADHD, masking is not a conscious choice to deceive others; it is often a deeply ingrained, unconscious survival strategy developed over a lifetime to conform to neurotypical expectations and avoid social judgment.

The diagnostic disparity in ADHD, where males are more frequently diagnosed due to their external, hyperactive symptoms, is partly explained by the fact that girls and women are more likely to develop these compensatory behaviors that obscure their underlying struggles.

A woman may meticulously maintain a façade of punctuality by building in extra time for everything, a strategy she developed to combat her innate time blindness and avoid the social consequences of being late.

Another might learn to pretend to take notes in a meeting to hide the fact that she is "zoning out" or has a "thousand-yard stare." These are just a few examples of the sophisticated coping mechanisms developed to appear "non-ADHD".

While a woman may be successful in hiding her struggles, the emotional and psychological cost of this performance is immense. The constant, exhausting effort to appear neurotypical is an invisible burden that leads to a lifetime of internalized shame, anxiety, depression, and a shattered sense of self-worth. Research confirms that girls are more likely to mask their symptoms than boys, and this can lead to significant negative consequences on their mental health, social functioning, and academic achievement.

A woman may feel like a fraud or an impostor, constantly fearing that her "perceived failures" will be discovered and that she will be rejected for who she truly is. This fear of exposure can lead to chronic loneliness and a debilitating sense of not being able to be one's authentic self. The longer a woman masks her symptoms, the more difficult it can be to find out who she really is after a diagnosis.

The Neurobiological Pain of Rejection Sensitive Dysphoria (RSD)

A particularly painful and debilitating manifestation of emotional dysregulation that is highly common in women with ADHD is Rejection Sensitive Dysphoria (RSD). For a woman with ADHD, a perceived social snub, a critical tone of voice, or a hint of disapproval is not just hurtful; it is an immediate, overwhelming emotional pain that can feel physically agonizing. Experts believe that the extreme pain of RSD is a real, physiological response in the ADHD brain, rooted in a distinct functioning of brain regions responsible for emotional processing and regulation.

An overactive amygdala (the brain's alarm system) combined with a less active prefrontal cortex (the brain's emotional "brakes") can lead to an immediate and overwhelming emotional response with little time for a thoughtful, inhibited reaction.

The hypersensitivity of RSD is often a direct result of a lifetime of chronic negative feedback and a learned expectation of rejection. As girls, their ADHD symptoms of impulsivity, emotional over-reactivity, or disorganization were inconsistent with societal expectations, making them a target for criticism or social judgment from family, peers, and teachers. These early traumatic experiences, which are often unpredictable and repeated, can trigger primitive survival mechanisms in the brain, leaving a girl's resilience chipped away.

An expectation of future social adversity is created, and a woman may interpret a partner's neutral or ambiguous behavior as an intentional sign of rejection, which can trigger an overreaction that ironically can compromise the relationship.

To avoid the profound emotional pain of RSD, a woman may develop sophisticated compensatory behaviors like people-pleasing and perfectionism. A woman may constantly try to accommodate the needs of others while neglecting her own, a strategy that is both exhausting and unsustainable.

However, the painful feedback loop continues, as a woman's emotional volatility may be seen as a "melodramatic overreaction" by others, which further invalidates her pain and reinforces her sense of being unworthy. A combination of a lifetime of negative feedback and the belief that she can do "nothing right" can lead to despair, which is why studies suggest women with untreated ADHD are more likely to make suicide attempts and self-harm than their male counterparts.

The Erosion of Connection: Loneliness and the Social Toll

The same executive function and emotional regulation challenges that affect a woman's home life also create significant barriers in her broader social dynamics and friendships. For women, social connections are central to their well-being, and a lack of a well-developed support network can be a significant source of pain.

Research indicates that women with ADHD have a harder time forming and maintaining friendships, which can lead to feelings of loneliness and a painful sense of "never fitting in". A study on girls with ADHD found that those with hyperactive/impulsive symptoms were "socially rejected," while those with the quieter, inattentive subtype were "socially neglected," or simply left out of social groups altogether. These patterns, which are deeply painful for women who have a greater need for social acceptance than men, persist into adulthood.

A woman's struggles to meet neurotypical social expectations are often rooted in her ADHD symptoms. She may have difficulty with active listening, where her mind wanders or "zones out" during conversations, leading her friends to feel unheard or unprioritized.

A woman with ADHD may also struggle to suppress the urge to interrupt in conversation because she fears she will forget what she wanted to say. An inability to consistently meet these social expectations, such as showing up on time for social commitments or curbing her tendency to talk too much, can lead to social rejection or the perception of being rude, which can take a significant toll on a woman's self-esteem.

The stress of these social challenges is heightened for women with ADHD, as they are less likely to have a well-developed social support network, which serves as a vital buffer against stress and emotional turmoil for neurotypical women.

Healing from a Lifetime of Shame: The Path to Self-Acceptance

The social cost of living with ADHD, the shame, the loneliness, the pain of rejection sensitivity, is a heavy burden to carry, but it is not a permanent one. Healing from a lifetime of masking requires a fundamental shift in a woman's relationship with her neurodiversity. It is a journey of moving from a place of self-blame and self-loathing to a place of self-compassion and genuine self-acceptance.

A woman can begin to cultivate a more compassionate and accepting relationship with her neurodiversity by actively challenging the negative narrative she has internalized. She must learn to recognize that her struggles are not a reflection of her character but a result of her brain's unique wiring.

A woman can reframe her struggles from "What's wrong with me?" to "My brain works differently, and what can I do to support it?" This compassionate stance is a powerful first step in dismantling the shame that has been a constant companion. A woman's emotional volatility and difficulties with self-regulation, for example, can be reframed not as a sign of being "dramatic" but as a neurobiological reality that can be managed with the right tools.

Healing from the social cost of ADHD also requires a proactive approach to communication and connection. A woman can start by gently educating her loved ones about her ADHD, helping them understand that her behaviors are not a reflection of a lack of care but a result of a different brain wiring. By sharing resources and explaining the "why" behind her struggles, she can foster empathy and reduce the blame and misunderstanding that so often arise from these situations.

A woman's partner, for example, can be educated about how RSD works so that they can offer gentle reassurance and validate her feelings, even if they don't fully understand them.

Finally, a woman must actively seek out and find communities that are validating and affirming. Isolation amplifies distress, and a lack of a strong social network can be particularly damaging for women with ADHD.

A woman can connect with others who share her experience through online forums, support groups, or coaching groups that provide encouragement, understanding, acceptance, and support. This practice of finding her community is an essential step towards healing from a lifetime of masking and building a foundation of genuine self-acceptance and belonging.

When a woman with ADHD finds a community where she can feel seen and accepted for who she is, she can begin to heal from a lifetime of hurts and learn to embrace her authentic self.

The journey of healing from the social cost of ADHD is not a linear one, and there will be days when the inner critic gets loud and the shame resurfaces. The true strength lies not in achieving perfection, but in a woman's ability to consistently return to her toolkit of self-compassion, re-engage with her strategies, and approach each challenge with curiosity and kindness. You now have the blueprint to navigate a challenging social landscape with greater inner stability, resilience, and strength, giving you a powerful foundation for building a life of authentic connection and genuine self-acceptance.

CHAPTER 5:

REDEFINING BALANCE:
INTEGRATING LIFE AREAS WITH ADHD

For a woman with ADHD, a truly balanced life is not about achieving neurotypical perfection; it is about honoring her unique needs and building a life that accommodates her brain's natural rhythms. This involves a conscious integration of the different areas of her life, ensuring that she is not pouring all her energy into one area while neglecting others. It is critical to recognize that her ADHD symptoms, such as the love of novelty and the capacity for hyperfocus, can be powerful assets when managed intentionally.

A balanced life means recognizing that a woman needs to refuel on weekends, and that her needs for self-care are not a luxury but a fundamental necessity for her well-being. It means being compassionate with herself when a strategy fails and understanding that the journey is one of continuous learning and adaptation. The final chapter provides a holistic approach to living, where a woman can integrate her personal needs, her relationships, and her professional aspirations into a harmonious system that is uniquely her own.

The Myth of Perfect Balance and the Neurobiological Reality

The concept of a "balanced life" is often portrayed as a serene, perfectly orchestrated state where every area, work, family, health, and personal life, receives an equal amount of attention at all times. For a woman with ADHD, whose brain is not designed for this kind of rigid, sustained equilibrium, chasing this ideal can be a fast track to exhaustion and shame.

The "do it all" expectation that women should excel in both the public and private spheres often leaves them feeling overwhelmed and undervalued, a struggle that is profoundly exacerbated by ADHD symptoms. Research shows women report higher levels of stress than men, largely due to the "work-life conflict" that arises when they are expected to meet the demands of both family and work life simultaneously.

A woman's brain, with its executive function deficits in planning, prioritization, and time management, is simply not equipped to flawlessly juggle every demand in a way that feels seamless to a neurotypical individual. Her natural energy cycles are often unpredictable, with periods of intense focus and surges of energy followed by sudden crashes of exhaustion, a pattern that makes consistent, linear progress difficult.

Attempting to force a rigid, neurotypical definition of balance onto a neurodiverse brain is not only ineffective but also a source of significant mental fatigue, a constant, conscious effort to manage internalized symptoms that drains a woman's energy reserves and makes her more susceptible to burnout.

Harnessing Your ADHD Superpowers: Hyperfocus and Novelty

A truly balanced life for a woman with ADHD is not about eradicating her symptoms but about learning to see them as a source of unique strengths and adaptive capabilities when managed with intention. Her neurodiversity comes with inherent strengths that can be harnessed for extraordinary output.

- **The Power of Hyperfocus:** Hyperfocus, often viewed as a double-edged sword, is a state of intense and prolonged concentration on a specific task or activity. While it can lead to the neglect of other responsibilities, it can also be a powerful tool for productivity and creativity when channeled intentionally. A woman's ability to get so engaged in a project that she is unaware of her surroundings can be an asset in fields that require deep concentration, such as writing, research, or programming. The key is to direct this superpower toward high-leverage, meaningful tasks, using external reminders and alarms to break out of a hyperfocused state and prevent a work-life imbalance.

- **The Advantage of Novelty-Seeking:** The ADHD brain's natural inclination toward novelty is a neurobiological reality tied to its dopamine reward system. While this can lead to impulsivity and a trail of unfinished projects, it can also be the engine of innovation and creativity. Many ADHD brains excel at seeing connections others miss and approaching problems from unexpected angles. This strength can be leveraged by pursuing creative or entrepreneurial endeavors that provide a constant flow of new ideas and stimulating challenges. A balanced life means a woman can honor her need for novelty by engaging in hobbies or projects that provide this kind of stimulation without letting them derail her long-term goals or responsibilities.

The Framework for an Integrated Life

An integrated life is one where your various needs, professional, personal, emotional, and social, are not seen as separate domains to be balanced but as interconnected parts of a holistic system. This is an intentional way of living that acknowledges that what you do in one area of your life directly impacts all the others.

- **Schedule and Boundaries:** A woman can build a life that accommodates her brain's natural rhythms by creating a flexible but structured schedule that prioritizes her unique needs. This means scheduling in "deep work" during her peak energy hours, but also intentionally scheduling in "low-energy" tasks during her more distractible or fatigued periods. Critically, she must also set firm boundaries to protect her energy reserves. Learning to say "no" to commitments that do not serve her and actively avoiding "energy vampires"—people, tasks, or social media activities that drain her—is a fundamental part of self-care and emotional well-being.

- **Proactive Self-Care as a Necessity:** For a woman with ADHD, self-care is not a luxury but a fundamental necessity for sustainable productivity and emotional well-being. Burnout is a state of chronic exhaustion driven by the daily demands of managing ADHD symptoms, and women are particularly susceptible due to the added pressure to conform to neurotypical standards. A woman can build resilience against burnout by prioritizing good sleep hygiene, as quality sleep is critical for attention and working memory. She can use regular physical exercise as a powerful antidote to mental fatigue, as it helps regulate dopamine levels and improves mood. Nourishing her body with a balanced diet rich in protein, healthy fats, and complex carbohydrates is also crucial for maintaining stable energy levels, which in turn supports sustained focus and emotional regulation. By consistently engaging in these practices, she is building a physiological buffer against the mental and emotional fatigue that often accompanies ADHD.

- **Continuous Learning and Adaptation:** The journey of a balanced life is not a linear one. There will be days when strategies fail, deadlines are missed, and the inner chaos feels overwhelming. The key to sustainable progress is not rigid adherence to a perfect system, but a compassionate, iterative process of review and adaptation. A woman can learn to reframe setbacks as a source of valuable data, asking herself: "What happened here? What was the friction point? What made this system hard to maintain today?" By approaching these moments with curiosity and kindness, she can learn from them and make small, strategic adjustments to her systems, making them more resilient and effective over time. This continuous cycle of learning, adapting, and refining is the true foundation of a well-organized and peaceful life.

This final chapter has provided a woman with a holistic approach to living, where she can integrate her personal needs, her relationships, and her professional aspirations into a harmonious system that is uniquely her own.

The mastery of these practical skills, from leveraging her strengths to building systems of support, is the ultimate validation of a truly balanced and integrated life with ADHD. By embracing her neurodiversity and recognizing that her optimal life is one she designs for herself, she can move from feeling powerless against her symptoms to a place of profound self-acceptance and empowerment. This intentional approach to living is the final and most important step in her journey.

Conclusion: Your Integrated Success

A roadmap for navigating the complex challenges of money and relationships has been provided in this book, demonstrating that a woman can move from a place of overwhelm to a place of integrated success. By confronting financial challenges head-on with systems that work for her ADHD brain, strengthening her communication with loved ones, and actively building a community that validates her experience, a woman can build a truly resilient and fulfilling life. The mastery of these practical skills is the ultimate validation of a truly balanced and integrated life with ADHD.

The Foundation of Practical Systems: Working with Your Brain

For women with ADHD, the struggles with finances and relationships are not a reflection of their intelligence or character; they are a direct result of core ADHD symptoms that profoundly impact daily functioning. Executive function deficits, particularly in areas like planning, organization, impulse control, and emotional regulation, make managing these two vital areas of life feel like an impossible task. The result is a persistent feeling of being overwhelmed and a consistent struggle to navigate adulthood in a way that feels seamless to a neurotypical individual.

The financial toll of these struggles is a measurable phenomenon known as the "financial ADHD tax," a lifelong cost that can significantly impact a woman's long-term financial health. Research from a 2020 study found that between the ages of 25 and 30, adults with ADHD show considerably slower growth in income and savings and often remain financially dependent on their families. By age 30, a projected retirement gap for a person with ADHD could be as much as 40% less net worth in the best-case scenario, potentially ballooning to 64% less when accounting for inconsistent saving patterns, a hallmark of the condition. A primary driver of this is impulsivity, a neurobiological difficulty in delaying gratification that leads to spontaneous purchases and a lack of savings.

Another significant factor is time blindness, which is a difficulty in accurately perceiving the passage of time that leads to late payments, accumulating fines, and a feeling that deadlines appear out of nowhere. The work in this book has provided a woman with the tools to confront these challenges head-on with systems that work for her ADHD brain, such as using automation and visual budgeting apps to bypass deficits in planning and organization.

A woman's relationships are also a mirror for her underlying ADHD symptoms. Communication, in particular, can be a major source of friction, as her mind may wander during conversations or she may impulsively interrupt, leading a partner to feel unheard and unprioritized. A particularly difficult dynamic can emerge when a neurotypical partner unintentionally takes on the role of a taskmaster to manage shared household responsibilities, leaving the ADHD partner feeling like a scolded child.

To overcome these hurdles, a woman has been equipped with intentional communication strategies like using "I" statements to express her feelings without blame and leveraging visual aids like a whiteboard chore chart to externalize shared responsibilities. By building these external systems and intentional communication practices, a woman moves from a place of reactive chaos to one of proactive, collaborative partnership.

The Emotional Core of Integrated Success

The consequences of these financial and relational struggles are not just external; they create a pervasive and amplifying emotional burden. A lifetime of feeling misunderstood, coupled with a pattern of failures rooted in ADHD symptoms, can lead to a deep-seated belief that a woman is inadequate or "not good enough."

A woman with undiagnosed ADHD reported feeling that she was "actually a bad person... I was not an adequate human being." The constant pressure to meet impossible societal standards and the perpetual cycle of feeling overwhelmed and behind can erode a woman's self-esteem and feed a pervasive sense of shame.

A painful and debilitating manifestation of this emotional dysregulation is Rejection Sensitive Dysphoria (RSD), an extreme emotional responsiveness to perceived rejection or criticism that is highly common in women with ADHD. This profound hypersensitivity is fueled by a lifetime of internalizing struggles and the fear that her "perceived failures" will be discovered. A woman's emotional volatility and misinterpretations may be seen as a "melodramatic overreaction" by others, which further invalidates her pain and reinforces her sense of being unworthy.

The constant effort to "mask" her symptoms to conform to neurotypical standards is a major source of this emotional burden, and it can lead to chronic loneliness and a debilitating sense of not being able to be her authentic self. A woman may feel like an impostor, constantly fearing that her true self will be discovered and she will be rejected, a painful experience that reinforces the low self-esteem and shame that are so prevalent in women with ADHD.

The mastery of these practical skills, from managing finances with strategic systems to communicating with greater clarity, is a powerful antidote to this profound emotional burden. The mastery of these practical skills is the ultimate validation of a truly balanced and integrated life with ADHD.

The Empowerment of Community and Self-Acceptance

Healing from a lifetime of shame and self-blame requires a fundamental shift in a woman's relationship with her neurodiversity. It is a journey of moving from a place of self-loathing to a place of self-compassion and genuine self-acceptance. A woman can begin to cultivate a more compassionate and accepting relationship with her neurodiversity by actively challenging the negative narrative she has internalized.

She can reframe her struggles from "What's wrong with me?" to "My brain works differently, and what can I do to support it?" This compassionate stance is a powerful first step in dismantling the shame that has been a constant companion.

Healing from the social cost of ADHD also requires a proactive approach to communication and connection. A woman can start by gently educating her loved ones about her ADHD, helping them understand that her behaviors are not a reflection of a lack of care but a result of a different brain wiring. By sharing resources and explaining the "why" behind her struggles, she can foster empathy and reduce the blame and misunderstanding that so often arise from these situations.

Furthermore, a woman must actively seek out and find communities that are validating and affirming, as isolation amplifies distress and a lack of a strong social network can be particularly damaging for women with ADHD.

A study on girls with ADHD found that those with hyperactive/impulsive symptoms were "socially rejected" by peers, while those with the quieter, inattentive subtype were "socially neglected," or simply left out of social groups altogether. These patterns, which are deeply painful for women who have a greater need for social acceptance than men, persist into adulthood, reinforcing feelings of loneliness and a sense of never "fitting in".

A robust social support network can serve as a vital buffer against stress and emotional turmoil, a coping mechanism that women are more likely to rely on than men. This practice of finding her community is an essential step towards healing from a lifetime of masking and building a foundation of genuine self-acceptance and belonging.

Integrating the Five Pillars: The Holistic Whole

The journey through this guide has been about building a life that is not just manageable but truly integrated and fulfilling. A woman is now empowered to leverage her strengths, mitigate her challenges, and create a harmonious system that is uniquely her own. A truly integrated success is not about achieving neurotypical perfection; it is about honoring your unique needs and building a life that accommodates your brain's natural rhythms.

A seamless, integrated life is a product of all five books working in synergy. The organizational systems you have built in Book 1 provide a stable and predictable base for the complex skills of focus and emotional mastery. A woman who has a system for taming her digital world is better equipped to manage the digital distractions that derail her focus (Book 2).

A woman who has reduced her daily stressors through functional organization has more mental and emotional bandwidth to manage the intense feelings and emotional dysregulation that are so prevalent in ADHD (Book 4), and she is less likely to feel overwhelmed by minor inconveniences that can trigger a disproportionate emotional storm.

The mastery of these practical skills, from managing finances with strategic systems to communicating with greater clarity, is the ultimate validation of a truly balanced and integrated life with ADHD.

This book provides a roadmap for navigating the complex challenges of money and relationships, demonstrating that a woman can move from a place of overwhelm to a place of integrated success. By confronting financial challenges with systems that work for her ADHD brain, strengthening her communication with loved ones, and actively building a community that validates her experience, a woman can build a truly resilient and fulfilling life. The mastery of these practical skills is the ultimate validation of a truly balanced and integrated life with ADHD.

Reflection Questions

- This part discusses the "ADHD tax" on finances and relationships. What is one practical system you can put in place to reduce the financial "tax" (e.g., using a single-purpose account, automating bill payments)?

- The book encourages gentle education about ADHD with loved ones. What is one thing about your ADHD brain that you can share with a partner or close friend to foster empathy and reduce misunderstanding?

- How can finding a validating and affirming community help you heal from the social toll of ADHD?

OVERALL CONCLUSION:

THE EMPOWERED WOMAN WITH ADHD

The journey through this five-book series has been an in-depth exploration of the multifaceted experience of ADHD in women. It has been a process of peeling back the layers of misconception and shame to reveal a path to empowerment and self-mastery. This guide has established that ADHD is not a deficit to be cured, but a unique operating system to be understood and strategically managed.

The analysis has provided a woman with a powerful toolkit for:

- **Self-Awareness:** A deep understanding of her brain's unique wiring, its rhythms, and its challenges, which is the foundation of all effective self-management.

- **Practical Strategies:** Concrete, evidence-based tools across all vital areas of life, designed to work with her ADHD brain, not against it.

- **Emotional Resilience:** The capacity to navigate intense feelings and cultivate an inner dialogue that supports her well-being.

- **System Building:** The ability to create external structures that compensate for internal challenges, freeing up mental energy for what truly matters.

- **Self-Compassion:** The crucial understanding that progress, not perfection, is the goal, and that kindness toward herself is the most powerful catalyst for sustainable change.

A woman is no longer merely coping with ADHD; she is actively crafting a life that is aligned with her unique strengths and values. The power lies in her newfound ability to recognize when she's struggling, refer back to her toolkit, re-engage with the strategies that work for her, and continuously review, adapt, and iterate her approach. She is now an Empowered Woman with ADHD, and she possesses the knowledge, skills, and mindset to navigate her world with greater clarity, purpose, and peace. She can embrace her neurodiversity, celebrate her unique gifts, and continue to build the extraordinary life she is capable of living.

HERE'S ANOTHER BOOK BY VIVIAN WHITMORE
THAT YOU MIGHT LIKE

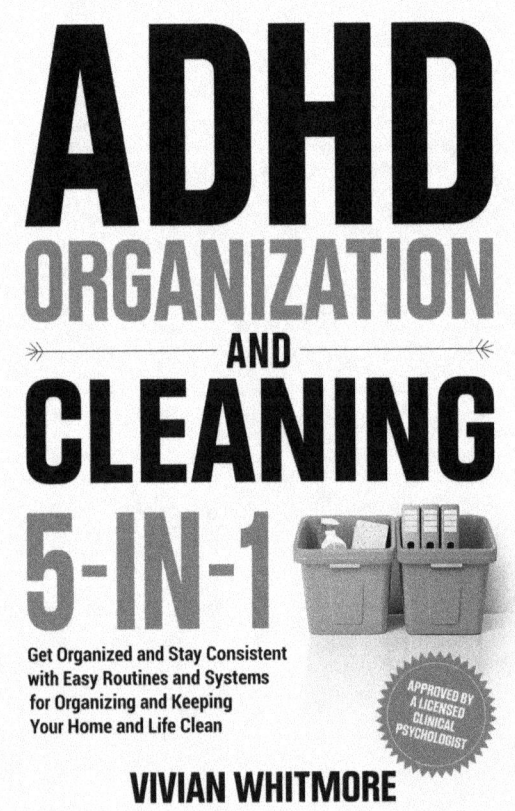

Claim Your Free Bonus

As a thank you for reading, I've put together a powerful digital bonus pack to help you apply what you've learned — even if you only have a few minutes a day.

 Inside you'll find:

✔ Quick-access emotional reset tools
✔ A printable clarity map for focus and purpose
✔ 30 powerful journaling prompts
✔ Daily progress & reflection trackers
✔ A mini affirmation deck for calm and confidence

Access below to download your full bonus pack:

https://livetolearn.lpages.co/vivian-withmore-women-with-adhd-5-in-1-paperback/

Or, scan the QR code

REFERENCES

1. Par, Inc. "The Relationship Between Adult ADHD and Executive Function Deficits." https://www.parinc.com/learning-center/par-blog/detail/blog/2025/03/11/the-relationship-between-adult-adhd-and-executive-function-deficits

2. CHADD. "Why ADHD Is More Challenging for Women." https://chadd.org/attention-article/why-adhd-is-more-challenging-for-women/

3. Frontiers in Psychology. "ADHD and Sex Hormones in Females: A Systematic Review." https://www.frontiersin.org/journals/global-womens-health/articles/10.3389/fgwh.2025.1549028/full

4. PubMed Central. "Cognitive and perceptual load have opposing effects on brain network efficiency and behavioral variability in ADHD." https://pmc.ncbi.nlm.nih.gov/articles/PMC10727773/

5. Medical News Today. "ADHD and organization: Strategies to improve organization." https://www.medicalnewstoday.com/articles/adhd-and-organization

6. PubMed Central. "Learning and Memory Impairments With Attention-Deficit/Hyperactivity Disorder." https://pmc.ncbi.nlm.nih.gov/articles/PMC11081185/

7. ADD.org. "Executive Function Disorder & ADHD." https://add.org/executive-function-disorder/

8. Verywell Mind. "Multitasking." https://www.verywellmind.com/multitasking-2795003

9. Frontiers in Human Neuroscience. "The Effects of Working Memory Load on Auditory Distraction in Adults With Attention Deficit Hyperactivity Disorder." https://www.frontiersin.org/journals/human-neuroscience/articles/10.3389/fnhum.2021.771711/full

10. ADDitude Magazine. "ADHD, Masking, and Impostor Syndrome." https://www.additudemag.com/adhd-masking-signs-consequences-solutions/

11. Additude. "Why ADHD Is More Challenging for Women." https://www.additudemag.com/gender-differences-in-adhd-women-vs-men/

12. Medical News Today. "ADHD and organization: Strategies to improve organization." https://www.medicalnewstoday.com/articles/adhd-and-organization

13. LearningRx Brain Training. "Why Is Organization So Hard for People with ADHD?" https://www.learningrx.com/reston/why-organization-is-so-hard-adhd/

14. Psychiatrist.com. "3 Ways ADHD Makes Romantic Relationships More Challenging." https://www.psychiatrist.com/news/3-ways-adhd-makes-romantic-relationships-more-challenging/

15. Additude. "Hormonal Changes in Women with ADHD: 4 Gaping Holes in Research." https://www.additudemag.com/hormonal-changes-in-women-adhd-research/

16. The ADHD Centre for Women. "ADHD and Hormones in Women: Understanding the Link." https://adhdcentreforwomen.com/elementor-3748/

17. Monash University. "How hormones and the menstrual cycle can affect women with ADHD: 5 common questions." https://www.monash.edu/medicine/news/latest/2023-articles/how-hormones-and-the-menstrual-cycle-can-affect-women-with-adhd-5-common-questions

18. ADDitude Magazine. "PMS and ADHD: How the Menstrual Cycle Intensifies Symptoms." https://www.additudemag.com/adhd-and-periods-menstrual-cycle-hormones/

19. Grantome. "R01-MH119119-01A1." https://grantome.com/grant/NIH/R01-MH119119-01A1

20. ADD.org. "PMDD and ADHD." https://add.org/pmdd-and-adhd/

21. Healthline. "ADHD and Hormonal Changes in Women." https://www.healthline.com/health/adhd/adhd-and-hormonal-changes-in-women

22. CHADD.org. "Frenzied, Frazzled, and Overwhelmed: The Interaction of Hormones and ADHD in Women in Midlife." https://chadd.org/adhd-news/adhd-news-adults/frenzied-frazzled-and-overwhelmed-the-interaction-of-hormones-and-adhd-in-women-in-midlife/

23. Everynow.com. "Brain Fog or ADHD: How Perimenopause Can Make Symptoms Worse." https://www.evernow.com/learn/brain-fog-or-adhd-how-perimenopause-can-make-symptoms-worse

24. Pauz Health. "Estrogen, Executive Function & ADHD: The Untold Story of Women's Brains." https://pauz.health/blog/estrogen-executive-function-adhd-the-untold-story-of-womens-brains

25. YouTube. "ADHD & Hormones: The Impact on Women's Brains and Lives with Dr. David Chapman." https://www.youtube.com/watch?v=oCltf1A0DDA

26. Trinity Health Michigan. "Ask a Doc: Females, ADHD and Perimenopause/Menopause." https://www.trinityhealthmichigan.org/blog-articles/ask-doc-females-adhd-perimenopausemenopause

27. Relational Psych. "ADHD and Hormones in Women." https://www.relationalpsych.group/articles/adhd-and-hormones-in-women

28. PubMed. "DAT1 and DRD4 genes involved in key dimensions of adult ADHD." https://pubmed.ncbi.nlm.nih.gov/25555995/

29. Growing Therapy. "What Is Self-Compassion." https://growtherapy.com/blog/what-is-self-compassion/

30. The Center for ADHD. "The ADHD Burnout Cycle: Understanding Symptoms, Causes, and Recovery." https://www.usa.edu/blog/adhd-burnout-understanding-symptoms-and-recovery-methods/

31. Simply Psychology. "Rejection Sensitivity In ADHD Relationships." https://www.simplypsychology.org/rejection-sensitive-dysphoria-relationships.html

32. The ADHD Centre. "Emotional Dysregulation in ADHD." https://add.org/emotional-dysregulation-adhd/

33. The ADHD Centre. "DBT for ADHD." https://www.charliehealth.com/treatment-modalities/dialectical-behavior-therapy/dbt-for-adhd

34. The ADHD Centre. "ADHD and Self-Compassion." https://chadd.org/attention-article/adhd-and-self-compassion/

35. The ADHD Centre. "The Five Pillars of Self-Compassion." https://self-compassion.org/what-is-self-compassion/

36. Mi-Psych. "The Benefits of Self-Compassion." https://mi-psych.com.au/the-benefits-of-self-compassion/

37. True Peace Center. "The Surprising Science Behind Self-Compassion." https://www.truepeacecenter.com/news/the-surprising-science-behind-self-compassion-and-why-it-actually-works

38. ADHD BC. "The Impact of ADHD on Adult Life." https://adhdbc.ca/blog/the-impact-of-adhd-on-adult-life-navigating-work-relationships-and-self-care

39. Gallup News. "Women Still Handle Main Household Tasks in U.S." https://news.gallup.com/poll/283979/women-handle-main-household-tasks.aspx

40. BYU ScholarsArchive. "Household Labor, Gender Roles, and Family Satisfaction." https://scholarsarchive.byu.edu/context/facpub/article/4865/viewcontent/Household_Labor__Gender_Roles__and_Family_Satisfaction.pdf

41. United Way NCA. "Gender Norms." https://unitedwaynca.org/blog/gender-norms/

42. Cleveland Clinic. "Executive Dysfunction." https://my.clevelandclinic.org/health/symptoms/23224-executive-dysfunction

43. ResearchGate. "The Neurobiological Profile of Girls with ADHD." https://www.researchgate.net/publication/390030819_Exploring_the_Experiences_of_Women_with_ADHD_in_Professional_Settings_A_Qualitative_Study

44. Investopedia. "The Financial Challenges of ADHD—And How To Overcome Them." https://www.investopedia.com/financial-challenges-of-adhd-11775648

45. ADD.org. "ADHD Money Management: Financial Success And Stability." https://add.org/adhd-friendly-financial-management-yes-and-its-not-what-you-think/

46. ADDitude Magazine. "Rejection Sensitivity Dysphoria." https://www.additudemag.com/rejection-sensitivity-women-adhd/

47. WebMD. "Rejection Sensitive Dysphoria." https://www.webmd.com/add-adhd/rejection-sensitive-dysphoria

48. ADDitude Magazine. "Women with ADHD: Mental Fatigue, Internal Hyperactivity, Emotional Dysregulation." https://www.additudemag.com/women-with-adhd-mental-fatigue-internal-hyperactivity-emotional-dysregulation/

49. ADDitude Magazine. "The Link Between ADHD and Hormones." https://www.additudemag.com/gender-differences-in-adhd-women-vs-men/

50. PMC. "The Neurobiological Profile of Girls with ADHD." https://pmc.ncbi.nlm.nih.gov/articles/PMC3534724/

51. Johns Hopkins University. "The Neurobiological Profile of Girls with ADHD." https://pure.johnshopkins.edu/en/publications/the-neurobiological-profile-of-girls-with-adhd-4

52. The ADHD Centre for Women. "ADHD and Hormones: Understanding the Link."
https://adhdcentreforwomen.com/elementor-3748/

53. "ADHD and organization | Proven strategies to simplify your life"
https://www.tiimoapp.com/resource-hub/adhd-at-work-how-to-get-organized